WHY BAD THINGS HAPPEN TO GOOD INVESTMENTS

WHY BAD THINGS HAPPEN TO GOOD INVESTMENTS

HOW YOU CAN INVEST SUCCESSFULLY

William T. Hepburn

First Edition

HCM Press
Prescott, AZ

Printed in the United States of America.

HCM Press
2069 Willow Creek Road
Prescott, AZ 86301

Library of Congress Cataloguing-in-Publications Data

Hepburn, William T.

      Why Bad Things Happen to Good Investments: How You Can Invest Successfully / William T. Hepburn – 1st ed.

        p.   cm
        Includes index.

        ISBN: 978-0-692-06903-5

I've watched people lose money they took decades to save, retired friends forced back to work, and parents compelled to move in with their children, all because they blindly followed traditional financial advice not knowing that most financial advice only works some of the time. This book shines a light onto traditional financial advice, so you can decide when to follow it and when not to and help save you from suffering the same fate as many investors who did not know how to keep bad things from happening to their good investments.

CONTENTS

PREFACE

In an investment career spanning four decades, my primary objective has been to ensure that my clients never have a terrible life-changing financial event, such as what happened to many investors in 2001 or 2008. Stock market crashes, bankruptcies and runaway inflation are the types of problems investors like yourself must dodge to be successful over the long haul.

This may sound strange, but investors rarely buy really bad investments. Of course, there are some stinkers out there, but many more people lose money in good investments gone sour than ever lose money to crooks and bad investments.

The infamous Bernie Madoff will forever be known as one of the greatest scamsters of all time. However, even Bernie Madoff was successful for his clients for 11up to 30 years before resorting to fraud around 1990. Losses, combined with an ego that would not allow Madoff to admit to those losses, changed Madoff's work from legitimate investments to a scheme that ruined lives.

Madoff lost investors an estimated $18 billion, but that was pocket change compared to the trillions of dollars lost in major market declines such as 2000-03 or 2007-09.

Prior to Madoff, one of the most egregious scandals involved the collapse of Enron, a large energy company. Enron's collapse was blamed upon Arthur Andersen, one of the Big Five accountancy partnerships in the world, which should have, but did not, report Enron's fabricated financial reports. Both Enron and Arthur Anderson ended up bankrupt because of the scandal.

When teaching college classes, I often ask how many students think Enron was a bad investment? Since Enron's stock price went to zero in the collapse of 2001, almost every hand in the class will shoot up. Yet

Enron made over 1,100 percent profit for people who got out at the right time; so even Enron started out as a good investment.

What makes the difference between someone who doubled, tripled or had even greater gains in Enron stock and those who lost everything? The losers simply did not have a plan for when things change. The successful investors planned for change, not knowing anything about Enron's fortunes, but realizing that change is inevitable.

The one thing that is as certain as death and taxes is that things are going to change. Constant cycles rule the investment world. So why do investors buy investments without giving any thought to the ever-changing market environment? In particular, why do investors plunk down a significant portion of their savings on investments when so many of them end up disappointing their owners?

Part of the reason is the thorough sales job from the well-polished marketing machine Wall Street has built. Wall Street's salesmen do such a good job of convincing investors that the offering they are considering is so solid, so timely, and priced so right that investors make their decision based upon that investment being right for them right now. In following this path, they fail to look ahead and consider what might happen to their new investment if the markets change, as they inevitably will.

Certainly, the Wall Street sales machine isn't much help in determining prospective problems with an investment. In fairness to the brokerage community, they are just human and can't know what might possibly happen years down the road. Prospectuses are not much help to the average reader either, using terms that are hard for the average investor to relate to despite fulfilling the legal requirement to disclose risk. To most of us, disclosures are just words while real losses, when they occur, are often felt like gut punches.

So, if you are like most investors, the problem remains the same; how to protect yourself from life-altering financial events with little help from Wall Street or industry regulators.

It is my hope that this book can provide some solutions to that problem. Although the focus of this book is on stock or equity fund investing, the principles and insights presented here can be applied to almost any financial investment.

May all your investments stay good ones.

ACKNOWLEDGEMENTS

Most of the knowledge and wisdom that is contained in this book is not my own. I have had many mentors, teachers, and friends in my 30+ years in this business, who each added to and shaped my investment worldview. I want to thank them all.

Without Linda Ferentchak of Financial Communications Associates (ActiveManagersResource.com), encouraging me to put my ideas together in this book and assisting with organizing and editing the final publication, this book might never have moved from my wish list to reality. Linda's knowledge of the financial services industry, and proactive management in particular, was invaluable in keeping this book going in the direction that was intended. You make me look good, Linda! Thank you, thank you, thank you.

At one point in my career I had more than 20 engineers as clients who were all extremely detailed in both training and temperament, because lives literally depend upon their work being exact. I was often asked about nuances and obscure facets of investing that in my laziness or haste to get to the next task I might never have looked at myself. Each time I would have to research these topics, I became better at advising clients, and that process made me into the expert that I am today. To all the engineers in the world, thank you.

Sir John Templeton, founder of the Templeton family of funds, now part of the Franklin mutual fund complex had a wonderful way to find value in markets. He had long been an idol of mine for his investing acumen, his philanthropy, and his spiritual leadership. Sir John also became a mentor to me in 1997 when I was invited to meet privately with him at his home in Nassau, Bahamas.

My brother, Mal, a retired banker, showed me how important it was to avoid losing money, and his philosophy led to the development of my current risk-averse style of investing.

I will be long indebted to Michael Price and Lee Harris of Price Capital Management who so graciously and freely shared their wisdom and keen market insight as well as their skills in using the FastTrack charting program.

Robert Kiyosaki introduced me to some of the most inspiring people he knew at a meeting of his. That meeting produced many of the ideas for his mega-best seller **RICH DAD, POOR DAD**. I wish I had a nickel for every book Robert has sold.

Eric Schwartz, founder of Cambridge Investment Research, allowed me to be one of his first investment representatives at Cambridge, and he showed me that great clarity could spring from a spiritual foundation to business.

Tom McClellan, publisher of the **MCCLELLAN MARKET REPORT** (McOscillator.com), may be the greatest visual trader I have ever met, and I continue to get great insights from him.

Market historian Rob Powers was the first to point out to me the generational nature of stock market cycles, something I might not have noticed without his direction.

Brian Hayward, former manager of the Invesco Telecom fund, provided me with a huge insight on mutual fund management which led me to create the market niche for my business that it thrives in to this day, filling the gap between what clients want and the type of management that mutual funds are structured to deliver.

To the incredibly bright John McClure of ProfitScore, Paul Schatz of Heritage Capital in Connecticut, genius-quant Ian Naismith, Don Beasley and his down-home way of describing investments, Jerry Wagner, who I have watched build a big business at Flexible Plan Investments, and the many other members of the National Association of Active Investment Managers, who have helped my knowledge and wisdom grow and my business to flourish, my thanks.

I learned a lot about running mutual funds by rubbing shoulders at many meetings over the years with mutual fund managers and executives, such as Dave Wright of Sierra Funds, Ralph Doudera of Spectrum and Hundredfold Funds, Greg Morris of Stadion Funds, Dan Hornbaker, Kristine Warner and Carl Resnick of Rydex Funds, Matt Connors, Jeff Omdahl and Bill Van Hoof of Profunds, Steve Blumenthal and Jason Wilder of CMG Mutual Funds, and Marty Kerns of Kerns Capital Management and the KCM Macro Trends Fund.

I would not be the expert I am today without learning from many independent money managers such as Jim Applegate of Financial Services Advisory; Ken Graves of Capital Research Advisors; Roger Schreiner of Schreiner Capital Management; Dave Lucca, founder of the Rhodes, Lucca investment firm and a genius at marketing; Ted Lundgren of Hg Capital Advisors; Cliff Montgomery; Brenda Wenning in Boston; Dave Wagner of Active Investment Management; Colleen Chandler of VennWell, and Dave Moenning of Sowell Management Services. Thank you all for sharing your knowledge, skills, and wisdom with me over the years.

INTRODUCTION

ABOUT THE BOOK

My goal in writing this book is simple, to make you a better investor through some straightforward insights, tips and techniques that will, hopefully, lead you to own a portfolio that is not only diversified, but *effectively* diversified. There is a big difference.

You'll find in these pages a simple, yet practical overview of the financial markets, including how to deal with the relentless nature of the cycles that devastate many investments. You will discover ways that Wall Street has the deck stacked against you, and I will show you how to recognize the constant propaganda assault they use to reinforce their messages, so you can insulate your portfolio from their intentions for your money.

When some folks see the dark corners of Wall Street that I shine a light on in this book, they might think "Why bother to invest at all?" So, I'll discuss why you should put up with all the Wall Street pickpockets and how to use Wall Street without being taken in by them. There are many investment pitfalls. I'll alert you to some of the most common investor mistakes and which are the most expensive for investors to make, and, naturally, I tell you what steps you should take to avoid them. There are also outright scams out there and I enjoy exposing those as I go.

Part of the educational process in this book will be to help you identify what type of investor you are. This is important because it provides a lens through which you can evaluate any investment for its appropriateness for you personally. What might be a fine investment for others might not be right for you. One size does not fit all. I'll also give you some tips on how to find the right kind of professional help you need to best fit your personal circumstances.

We will talk about different types of investments and in what circumstances you should use one or another. I'll provide some basic investment planning advice along the way, such as the problems that can be created by being overly conservative with your money. I will show you a better way to approach capital preservation than just burying your money in the lowest-yielding instruments.

After laying some groundwork, we will look at a number of simple investment strategies and tactical tools that you can use even if you are not a math wizard. There will also be a discussion of effective diversification versus the ineffective diversification that most investors end up with. After reading this book, you will know what it takes for you to become a good investor.

If you find value in only one of the nuggets of wisdom in these pages, your investment in this book will pay off handsomely. My guess is that you will find a lot to relate to in the stories and insights discussed as you breeze through the chapters.

ABOUT THE AUTHOR

This is my first go at writing a book. In real life, I am a professional money manager and an off-Wall Street industry leader with over 30 years of experience. That experience includes riding through and surviving - more importantly, helping individuals like you survive - the Black Monday market crash in October 1987, several wars around the world, the 2000-03 bear market, the financial crisis of 2008, and other scary stuff. You could say I went to the School of Hard Knocks, because I learned how to be a better investor with each of those challenges.

My practical education began years before I entered this business. In fact, when someone asks me why I moved to the beautiful, cool mountains of Prescott, Arizona in 1986, I often break out my characteristic grin and respond, "impending poverty." Let me explain:

My career got its start as a business analyst for Dun & Bradstreet before enrolling in computer school in 1970. The Army snatched me up during the Vietnam Era and, as fate would have it, sent me to Alaska. Compared to what I had heard about Vietnam, Alaska sounded mighty good. I liked Alaska and the adventure it offered induced me to stay there when I was discharged in 1974.

I worked for a while doing systems analysis to computerize the financial management system for the Municipality of Anchorage, a job I was good at, but really did not enjoy at all. I saw the big bucks being made building the Alaska pipeline back then, so I quit my secure job with the government and became a professional snow shoveler on the pipeline. I worked the night shift at the Valdez Pipeline Terminal shoveling snow for 12 ½ hours a night. I was grateful for the deep snow of Valdez, because when we ran out of snow, we shoveled rock. On my time off, I learned that I could make as much money playing poker as I did on my paychecks. Life was prosperous!

My time on the pipeline gave me two things: One was enough money to get out of the 9 to 5 rut of living paycheck to paycheck. The second was knowing that I didn't want to do shovel work all my life.

The pipeline was finished about the time I wanted to sell my first home to get the equity, start buying rental properties and playing monopoly. Alaska flourished, and my net worth soared! I was a millionaire by the time I was 36. And I found myself broke by the time I was 38.

Back then I thought diversification meant owning some houses, some condos, and some multi-family units. When the oil markets collapsed in the mid-1980s, however, the economy in Alaska crashed too, and I began to see how short-sighted I had been.

Vacancies soared, rents dropped and soon I had a huge negative cash flow. I sold properties as fast as I could to feed the alligators, but it was no use. I lost my business and my house in the two-year, slow-motion real estate collapse, much like the one that happened in the U.S. following the financial crisis of 2008. Finally, I gave the last few properties back to the bank and climbed into an old used motorhome to look for a new place to live.

I was poorer but wiser and had learned a very expensive lesson about what diversification is and is not. In this book, you will hear me preach about *effective* diversification versus flawed diversification plans that are worse than worthless, they are dangerous to your financial health. My experience keeps this distinction vivid in my mind.

Real estate can be a great investment, and I own real estate today. My timing was bad during my Alaska experience and it cost me dearly. Such is life. Investors must understand that real estate is not without risks and should be only a part of one's investment portfolio. To have 100% of your holdings in real estate will produce ineffective diversification and high risk.

I broke into the securities side of the investment business (as opposed to the real estate or insurance sides) in 1987 as a municipal bond broker, selling mutual funds on the side. I practiced as a Certified Financial Planner™ for a dozen years, giving up that shingle in 2006 to focus solely on portfolio management.

In 1990, I began to teach about investments at Yavapai College, our local community college that now serves 11,000 students per year. Since 1990, several thousand students have taken my college classes and many of the examples, explanations and insights presented in this book were developed and refined for use in my classes.

As my sphere of influence expanded over the years, I was privileged to be invited to the home of one of my idols, legendary investor Sir John Templeton in Nassau, Bahamas. I was asked to manage mutual funds on two occasions and to become a board member for the National Association of Active Investment Managers (NAAIM), and was elected President of that organization in 2008. Among my initiatives NAAIM completed was development of a new market indicator, the NAAIM Index of Market Exposure, now closely followed and used in research and analysis by hundreds of websites, newsletter writers and market analysts. The NAAIM Index tracks the stock market exposure of active money managers, and, as newsletter writer Tom McClellan (MCCLELLAN MARKET REPORT, www.MCOscillator.com) has discovered, when the NAAIM Index is retreating and the major stock market indexes are rising, normally it is the NAAIM Index that is correct.

In recent years, I have conducted training sessions for other investment professionals, and at Mensa conventions around the country. Some really far out Mensa presentations I saw led me to become a futurist of sorts. I mean, who doesn't want a peek into the future? I had a long-held passion for future technologies and began to build them into my investment portfolios. I now run an investment strategy that focuses exclusively on investments in emerging technologies such as biotech, robotics, the Internet of Everything, etc.

In 2013, I began presenting seminars, including at Mensa gatherings, focusing on *Investing in Future Technologies*. Imagine the pressure when there are 150 geniuses in the audience, including scientists, researchers and engineers who work in the very industries I was discussing. When that adds up to more than 20,000 IQ points in the audience, they know more about some of the subjects than I do. Yikes! I've learned to give the audience a disclaimer that I am not a scientist or engineer, and only look at the investability of these companies. However, the Mensa presentations are stimulating, and I learn as much as I teach in those classes, sometimes more.

Although my practice is now exclusively portfolio management rather than the general financial planning and brokerage of stocks, funds, and annuities that my practice began with, as I talk to people I continue to find opportunities to pass along the wide-ranging insights I have gained over the years. Slowly, I realized that I needed to compile what I have learned in my 30+ years as a professional investment adviser into a book that will allow my knowledge to live on long after I am gone.

I like to write in plain English, in a style that I would use if you were sitting across the table from me, so I think you will find this book to have a low jargon content with concepts that are easy to grasp. Thanks for reading this far. I hope that you have as much fun reading the book as I had writing it.

Will Hepburn
Prescott, AZ

CHAPTER 1 - WHY YOU NEED TO BE AN INVESTOR

"There is an old saying on Wall Street that bulls can make money and bears can make money, but pigs and sheep get slaughtered. The way to protect yourself from these emotional risks is to have systems and the discipline to stick with them."

Will Hepburn

The number one reason to read this book is because you are disappointed with your investment results and you are looking for a better way to invest. Maybe you've reached the point of disillusionment, at which you are wondering if it makes sense to invest in the financial markets at all.

There's a lot of negative information in the chapters ahead about how the markets are stacked against the individual investor. You need to understand this reality because it will help you make better decisions and avoid some of the pitfalls you may have already encountered. ***However, investing also has tremendous value and is one of the best ways to grow your net worth and help you achieve financial security.***

An unavoidable fact of life is that you must invest your savings if you have financial objectives such as:

- Generate Income in Retirement
- Save for Retirement
- Reduce Income Taxes
- Grow Savings
- Never Lose Any Money

The last item on the list, never lose money, is a valid investment objective. Even burying your money in the back yard has risks such as worms eating it, someone finding your treasure map or dying without anyone else knowing where it is buried. Bank investments run the risk of being overtaken by inflation and taxes, reducing the purchasing power of the money you loan them.

If you think about it, the number of dollars you have is not nearly as important as what those dollars will do for you. If you stash enough in the bank to buy groceries and pay taxes for 20 years in retirement, and inflation is higher than your interest rate when you get to retirement, you may only be able to buy 19 years of groceries for your 20 years of retirement. This is a problem. This is where the stories come from of retirees forced to eat dog food because they run out of money earlier than planned, usually due to inflation in the costs of food, health care and taxes.

This table of historic CD returns after taxes and inflation shows what happened to the purchasing power of bank savings during what is considered the golden years of CD investing when double-digit CD interest rates were easy to find. The problem was not interest rates, but rate of inflation, which almost always leads interest rates.

Table 1 - Maintaining the purchasing power of your savings is a critical part of investing.

YEAR	CD INTEREST RATE	MAXIMUM FEDERAL INCOME TAX RATE	INFLATION	PURCHASING POWER
1979	11.44%	59%	13.3%	-8.61%
1980	12.94%	59%	12.5%	-7.19%
1981	15.79%	59%	8.9%	-2.43%
1982	12.57%	50%	3.8%	2.49%
2017	.25%*	35%	1.9%	-1.74%

Source: Federal Reserve Bulletin as reported by Oppenheimer Funds. Real CD Return is (CD Rate – Inflation Rate)-(CD Rate x Tax rate). Tax Rate is maximum Federal Income Tax. Inflation is the change in the Consumer Price Index as reported by the Bureau of Labor Statistics.
* Source: Bankrate.com 6-month CD.

In these environments, the banks gain purchasing power while investors lose it. So, doing nothing with your money, such as leaving it in low-yielding bank deposits or in stacks of cash, is just not a good option. Doing nothing is a plan to join the dog food eating crowd. If you don't want to go that direction, then as scary as it seems, you simply must invest your money, and hopefully invest it wisely. That is what this book is all about.

I often see investors frozen with fear about what may happen but overlooking what is actually happening.

Would you even think twice about investing if you knew that:

- ♦ Interest rates were about to shoot to over 10%?
- ♦ Bankruptcies and bank failures would soar?
- ♦ The stock market would drop more than 20% in one day?
- ♦ The President would be shot?
- ♦ The U.S. would be involved in a war?
- ♦ There would be rioting in the streets?

Most people would be unable to invest, worrying that these calamities would cause markets to crash and surely affect their investments, yet these were the conditions in the early 1980's at the beginning of the greatest bull market the U.S. financial markets have ever seen. By the end of the 1980s, the S&P 500 had risen 351% from its 1982 low, despite all these occurrences.

Today, we have similar issues to worry about:

- ♦ Natural disasters devastating large areas
- ♦ Unending wars in the Middle East
- ♦ The rise of Islamic terrorism
- ♦ Nuclear threats from North Korea
- ♦ Britain leaving the European Union
- ♦ Impending financial defaults in Greece and Italy

However, the markets just keep marching on. My point is that no matter how bad things seem right now, investors have faced similar fears since the beginning of time. The topics of the news articles might change, but they are no scarier than five or 10 years earlier.

Nothing was as scary as the cold war that raged for 40 years between the two biggest nuclear powers in the world, the United States and the USSR. If you are in my generation, you'll remember the A-bomb drills in school, where we all had to hide under our desks (like that would protect us from an atomic bomb). We even had those drills in the Midwest where there wasn't a Russian for 5,000 miles. That was the reaction of a scared nation. Yet the financial markets kept their dance of two steps forward, one step backward going through the whole 40 years.

The three most important rules of investing are:

- ♦ Don't lose your money
- ♦ Don't lose your money
- ♦ Don't lose your money

That may sound a bit facetious, but let's take a look at how many ways there are to lose money, or maybe just purchasing power.

In my classes, I often ask, "What investments have no risk?" It's a trick question, because the answer is none. If you can stretch your mind enough to look at risk in a different way you will notice that risk is the reason investments pay anything at all. If there were no risk there would be no reward for investing and we'd all be stuck stuffing money in mattresses because even banks wouldn't want it.

Risk may be a hard concept to grasp because we think of risk as being a single item, when, in fact, risks come in bunches. Just like you can snap a pencil in two, but might have a hard time snapping 10 at once, bunches of risks are more difficult to analyze and understand than one at a time.

There are **specific risks**, the kind that affect only a specific business, region or person. These are default risk, business risk, and event risk - the types of risk that impact only a single investment. The best protection from specific risks is diversification, so one default doesn't affect your whole investment portfolio.

Systemic risks affect a whole class of investments. Inflation risk, market risk, liquidity risk and currency risk are examples of this. The best protection is to have a combination of investments, so some will do well when systemic risks manifest themselves. If bonds will be hurt by inflation, also have some hard assets like gold or energy stocks that will do well during inflation. If stocks might be hurt by market risk, also own some bonds that often act counter to stocks. This kind of asset class diversification is how to protect yourself from systemic risks.

There is also emotional risk, the kind that compels you to do nothing with your money, in a fear-based paralysis. Or the kind that makes you greedily jump into the investment that has done so well that you have read about in the paper.

There is an old saying on Wall Street that bulls can make money and bears can make money, but pigs and sheep get slaughtered. The way to protect yourself from emotional risks is to have systems and the discipline to stick with them. And if you don't have systems yourself, hire someone who does to help you manage your money. It's not all that complicated – simply know the best type of advice for you (discussed in later chapters). However, you do have to take some action to get started.

Market risk may or may not happen at some time. Default risk may or may not happen at some time. But the two risks that are always happening are taxes and inflation. Don't overlook these constant risks while worrying about the "maybe" risks. Always take taxes and inflation into account when deciding if a particular investment will work for you.

Why should one take more than the minimum risk? Because $1.00 invested in 1928 is worth the following today:

♦ $19.89 invested in T-Bills (3.3% average)
♦ $ 71.11 invested in long-term Treasury Bonds (4.91% average)
♦ **$ 32,858.44 invested in Blue Chip Stocks (12.39% average)**

Source: Aswath Damodaran, adamodar@stern.nye.edu, Historical returns: Stocks, T.Bonds & T.Bills with premiums, January 1, 2017

These numbers represent the total returns of the investment categories listed from 1926 through 2016. Total return is the combination of interest or dividends paid, plus or minus any price change in the security, and in my opinion, is the best way to keep track of your investments.

Here is similar data presented graphically showing why people like

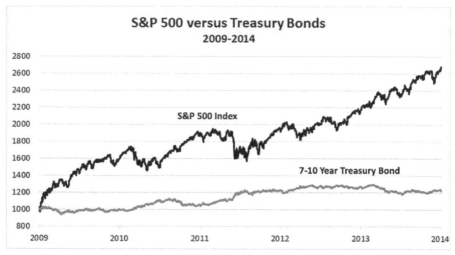

Figure 1 - Five-year comparison of the S&P 500 Index to the iShares 7-10 Year Treasury Bond ETF.

to invest in stocks.

When looking at the five-year period following the end of the 2007-09 bear market caused by the financial crisis, we see that the S&P 500 Index outperformed by about a 5 to 1 ratio. Reading this chart, it is easy to see that the place to invest was stocks compared to intermediate term treasury bonds

However, bonds have their place in an investment portfolio, too.

If we roll the five-year chart back another five years so it becomes a 10-year chart capturing the period of the financial crisis, owning the same iShares 7-10 Year Treasury Bond Exchange Traded Fund (IEF) could be a life savings saver in a full-blown bear market. These Treasuries delivered the same performance over the 10-year period from 3/9/04 to 3/7/2014 as stocks, but with a much, much smoother ride, meaning lower risk.

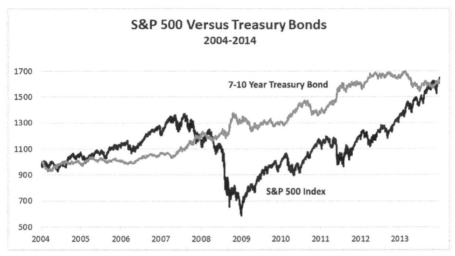

Figure 2 - Ten-year comparison of the S&P 500 Index to the iShares 7-10 Year Treasury Bond ETF.

Bonds won't always deliver this moderating performance, though. The period shown was a time of generally declining interest rates which causes bond prices to rise. Bond prices are expected to decline as rates begin to climb out of their 60-year bottom posted in 2016, leaving us the task of finding other investments that will balance out the market risk of owning stocks.

The point I would like to make in this chapter is don't be afraid to invest. Sure, there are risks to investing but they can be managed. Keep in mind that there are certain risks to not investing, too. If you don't want to manage your investments, hire someone to do that for you, but please **do not** do nothing with your money. Your family's financial future depends upon it.

Doing nothing is a strategy. It's not a good one, but it counts as a strategy. Just like the longest journey begins with a single step, by reading this far, you've already taken the first steps in your journey to better investment management. As you go through this book, make note of parts that seem to resonate with truth for you and decide to do them.

CHAPTER 2 - THE RISK OF BEING TOO CONSERVATIVE

"All things, investments and investment styles, cycle in and out of favor."

Legendary investor Sir John Templeton

My investment career began in a retirement town back in 1987. Several times early in that career I offered a prospective client a bond or mutual fund that I thought would best suit them, but got a reply along the lines of "with that much yield it must be too risky," and they would choose something delivering a lower yield believing it to be lower risk.

During the crash of 1987 and the bear market of 1990, I learned that the investments chosen by those clients usually did worse than my first investment recommendation, sometimes much worse. I learned right then that these unsophisticated investors were being too conservative for their own good, and that I needed to hold firm to my best investment recommendations – for the client's own good.

There are studies that show an investor's reaction to a loss is much stronger than their reaction to a similar gain, and my experience tells me those studies are correct. Given a choice, people will almost always choose what appears to be the more conservative option, even if it is not really the best choice for them.

THE MOST PRUDENT INVESTMENT MAY BE THE WRONG INVESTMENT

In my college classes, I tell the story of the man who inherited $100,000 at age 45 with his father's admonition to "take care of this money so you can be comfortable in retirement." Wanting to "take care of this money" as his father wished, on December 31, 1996, he invested in CDs earning 2.5% because they were a guaranteed investment. Over the next 20 years until his retirement at age 65, his money grew to $163,861. The income he could draw at 2.5% per year was $342 per month, not nearly enough to live on.

This man took the first half of his father's wishes "take care of this money" and interpreted it to mean "don't lose this money," which may or may not been his father's intent. However, the second part of his father's wish was "to be comfortable in retirement." He certainly missed that goal by being too conservative.

If instead, he had taken a moderate level of risk and invested in a portfolio that was 50% bonds and 50% stocks for the same 20 years ending Dec 30, 2016, he would have earned an average of 6.94% per year. His $100,000 would have grown to $282,240 and his annual income at that rate could have been $1,632 per month, enough to get by. (Source: FastTrack). By taking a moderate level of risk, he would have been able to fulfill his father's wishes.

Even if he had the misfortune of investing during the worst 20-year period in the history of his 50/50 portfolio, he would have earned an average annual return of 3.61% and his investment would be worth $203,250 at retirement. The income he could have earned at that rate would have been $611 per month, still not enough to live well on, but much better than a guaranteed investment over 20 years. (Source: Stock, Bonds, Bills and Inflation 1997 Yearbook, Ibbotson & Associates, Chicago.)

The moral of this story is that it is easy to get overly conservative and complacent thinking you are doing the most prudent thing, and lose sight of the real goal of investing, which is what your money can do for you later in life.

YOUR END GOAL IS TO BUILD PURCHASING POWER

Investors tend to worry about the big hairy risks like market crashes, but market crashes happen very infrequently. These same investors tend to lose sight of the risks that are with us all the time, like inflation and taxes. If you are not doing well enough to have more than the rate of inflation left after taxes, then your real return is negative. You are losing purchasing power.

We naturally tend to focus on the dollar value of our investments and forget that the real game is what those dollars can buy for us. Real return is what is left after taxes and inflation. The name of the investing game is to keep your eye not just on the dollars but on the real return you are getting.

Years ago, I came across this piece that puts the feeling of risk being all around us in perspective.

> *"It is a gloomy moment in the history of our country. Not in the lifetime of most men has there been so much grave and deep apprehension; never has the future seemed so incalculable as at this time. The domestic economic situation is in chaos. Our dollar is weak throughout the world. Prices are so high as to be utterly impossible. The political cauldron seethes and bubbles with uncertainty, war is in our future, and Russia hangs as usual, like a cloud, dark and silent on the horizon. It is a solemn moment. Of our troubles, no man can see the end."*

Sounds just like what's happening these days, doesn't it? But this piece was written for *Harper's Weekly Magazine* in October 1857. As bad as things seem today, they have always seemed bad at the time.

With all the fallout from recessions, low-cost labor from abroad, Islamic terrorism, and change coming from government actions (or inactions), it is easy to conclude that everything is going down the tubes. Change is often uncomfortable, but just because times are changing does not mean that life as we know it is coming to an end.

In the 1980s, everyone worried about Japan overtaking the US, until their economy came unglued, miring them down for the past 30 years. Today, a big bogeyman is China, and I expect that before too long the fragility of their command economy will cause a fate similar to Japan's.

The dollar was largely written off as going in the tank until the last few years when the whole world decided they liked the comfort of owning dollars during the worldwide financial crisis. Demand drove the dollar higher and it has stayed high.

The thing to keep in mind about currencies, is they cannot all go down at the same time. Currency values are measured against other currencies, not against a static benchmark. As one currency goes down, somewhere else at least one currency has to be going up.

In my experience, there are three factors that make a country's currency and its financial markets attractive to foreigners. They are:

1. Economic power
2. Political stability
3. Military might

No country can compete with the U.S. on all three of these points. A few countries might compete with us on one, but fall way back on the others; so, don't sell the U.S. or the dollar short. For over 200 years, anyone who has ever bet against the future of the United States has lost, and I don't expect that to change.

Our free market system is like a great river that, when encountering a boulder or other obstacle, adjusts, gathers its power and goes around, wrapping itself around the obstacle and making it a part of the river.

CASH CREATES OPPORTUNITIES

I had a discussion recently with a real estate investor who had trouble seeing the wisdom of keeping a lot of cash on hand when money market rates are so low. I pointed out that he was focusing on the wrong thing. First, a 1% money market rate is at least positive. If many investments begin to lose money, the money market fund is at least producing a positive return. But even that is not the main point.

The real value of money is not the number of dollars you have, but what you can buy with them. Economists refer to a change in purchasing power as the "real return" of an investment. Inflation can affect purchasing power in a negative way, but asset deflation – falling prices of stocks or real estate – affects purchasing power positively.

If you think about a money market fund that went from $100,000 to $101,000 over the past year, that is merely counting dollars and does not reflect purchasing power.

Consider that during a bear market, $101,000 in cash might be able to buy stocks that would have cost $130,000 earlier. In tight real estate market, $101,000 in cash might buy real estate that cost $150,000 a few years back. With this in mind, you then can appreciate the real value of the cash holdings. It is the relative value that cash holds when everything else is going down.

Now when someone tells you "cash is king" in declining markets, you will know what they mean – and it isn't the interest you can earn.

As I say several times in other sections of the book, this does not suggest that you should passively buy-and-hold cash, or cash equivalents like CDs. To be successful as an investor, you need to be ready to move from one asset class to another, buying low and selling high. That includes moving from a cash holding into stocks or real estate when they are down.

The late, legendary investor, Sir John Templeton, said "All things, investments and investment styles, cycle in and out of favor." This statement also applies to holding cash too long. At times it works just fine, but at other times one can be too conservative for their own good by doing so.

CHAPTER 3 - THE MOST EXPENSIVE MISTAKE – TRUSTING WELL-INTENTIONED BUT NAIVE ADVICE

"There is much more money lost to well-meaning but naïve financial advice than has ever been lost to crooks – even counting Bernie Madoff's record-breaking Ponzi scheme."

Will Hepburn

A little knowledge can be a dangerous thing. This is especially true in the investment world.

For more than 30 years, I have been telling people that history shows that there is much more money lost to well-meaning but naïve financial advice than has ever been lost to crooks – even counting Bernie Madoff's record-breaking Ponzi scheme.

In the past, I have focused this comment on advisers who were good mutual fund or annuity salesmen, but had no clue what really made the markets tick. Usually, they just repeat what someone else tells them without understanding the inter-market relationships that make investing more like a chess game than checkers. They fail to think things through to logical conclusions or have any idea about what might come next.

The investment world has an infinite number of variables and is so complex that no one person has ever mastered it perfectly, but the ability to look at the facts of what is actually happening now and deduce what may happen next is an incredibly valuable skill. If an adviser can't do that, what are you paying him for?

Many financial advisers will point to Morningstar ratings and sell you the mutual funds or annuities with the most stars. Of course, ratings are based primarily on past performance, and as the disclaimers all say, that has no bearing on whether you will make money going forward.

To give you an idea why listening to brokers say, "This one has done really well" is a very poor way to invest, let's look at the performance of top-rated "5 Star" funds versus below average "2 Star" funds during the tech collapse in 2000-2002.

On June 30, 2000, Morningstar gave 192 growth funds their top 5-star rating. Over the next two years those 192 funds returned average losses of 52%. Investors in those funds lost more than half of their money! Ouch! At the same time, Morningstar rated 218 value funds as below average with only 2 stars, which over the next two years produced average gains of 11%. Let's see. Losing half your money by following the industry leader in fund ratings versus 11% gains by ignoring them?

These results are completely backwards from what one would expect from the ratings alone. You see, ratings are based upon past performance and are not indicative of future performance. The disclaimers all say that, but investors have heard this so many times that they have become desensitized to the cautionary warnings.

Relying on ratings to make investment decisions is like driving your car by looking in the rearview mirror. Eventually there will be a curve in the road ahead and you will crash. The market threw ratings-following investors a curve in 2000-02 and many lost money because they relied upon past performance due to the buy-and-hold drumbeat from Wall Street. Consequently, they did not have a way to react to what the current market was doing. It happened again during the bear market of 2007-09.

THE FINANCIAL PLANNING CONFLICT

Have you ever wondered why it is so hard to find a fee-only financial planner willing to serve small clients or even middle-market savers? It is because no one can make a good living writing financial plans.

The vast majority of financial plans being done these days are loss leaders used to reel in commissioned or annual fee business. That is a huge conflict of interest, which renders most of the recommendations in those plans suspect.

In the mid-1990s, when I began practicing as a Certified Financial Planner™, I billed my time at $125 an hour for projects such as financial planning and research. I had a coming-of-age moment when I calculated that if I worked 40 hours per week at that rate, after I paid my three staffers, rent, split revenues with the brokerage firm through which I was licensed, and the many other expenses of being in this business, there would not be enough left to buy groceries.

If I had to survive on $125 per hour as a financial planner, I literally could not have made ends meet. Being a good financial planner, I recognized this issue for what it meant and realized that I had a choice to make. The only way to make ends meet as a financial planner would be to use the plan to steer clients to invest with me, which created a conflict of interest that bothered me just thinking about it.

Instead I stopped offering to produce formal financial planning documents and changed my business direction to become a fee-only portfolio manager. No more conflicts of interest. I just try to make my clients as much money as I can without causing them to lose sleep at night.

I know from experience that the process for a comprehensive financial plan takes many hours just to collect the data and enter it into the computer. The computer does its work in minutes, but then there is the time required to present the plan to the client and many more hours to actually implement it. Remember, with all the overhead costs in this industry, $125 per hour is about an effective minimum wage. Did you pay $125 times 8 hours for your plan? That is $1,000. If not, rather than getting the best possible financial plan for you in your particular circumstances, you probably were given a plan that was skewed toward benefiting the planner, and sometimes only the planner. Being paid a planning fee and commissions for business recommended by the plan is double dipping and a huge conflict of interest.

Financial planners are certified by the CFP Board of Standards, home to over 77,000 CFP®s. In 2002, we were in the midst of a 52% decline of the S&P 500 and an even deeper decline in the technology loaded Nasdaq Composite Index. Back then I practiced as a Certified Financial Planner™, so I approached the CFP Board of Standards suggesting additions to their curriculum. I asked them to move from the traditional buy-and-hold-is-the-only-way-to-go advice they promulgated and make CFPs aware that there is such a thing as proactive management of investments. Changes to allow CFPs to give advice to sell and move out of a declining market could have significantly reduced the huge losses investors incurred in the 2000-02 bear market and again in the 2007-09 financial crisis.

In 2002, the CFP Board had an authorized curriculum with over 1800 topics, only three of which were remotely related to active management. I had hoped my nudge would encourage them to include a few more active management subjects in their curriculum. I was told, politely, that the Board thought three out of 1800 was plenty. Disillusioned, I dropped my CFP® designation after a 12-year membership.

NEWS WILL MAKE YOU CRAZY

Fake News is the term used these days for the slanted fare presented by mainstream media. I have been aware of this dynamic within the investment industry for a couple of decades now. Laws preventing analysts from saying one thing to the public and another thing to their paying customers have only shifted the playing field a little bit. The practice is still rampant.

We are all generally aware that big institutions try to manipulate us individuals down here on Main Street. Governments spin the news in the way that will get the most votes on election day. Energy companies do it, the health care industry does it, and of course Wall Street institutions do it. For Wall Street the reason is money - your money.

Most of these national institutions, many whose names you would recognize are in the business of creating new issues of stocks, bonds, mutual funds and other financial derivatives. They make much more money creating new product than they make from the retail investor dealings you may know them for. For them to be able to sell all these new products there needs to be buyers ready and waiting. That is where you come in. You are the buyer.

These financial institutions can't make much money unless they have your money to work with, so the last thing they want is for you to cash out and leave. This is one reason why brokerage firms' buy recommendations outnumber their sell recommendations, often by a ratio of 50:1. They want you to buy, buy, buy and if they had their way, you would never, ever sell.

Buy recommendations are only one tool of Wall Street. Their propaganda machine also generates so many great investment myths – truisms that turn out to be less than right when examined closely. Like most myths, many begin with a bit of truth, but end up inferring much that may not be true.

In 1997, I was working on coordinating a *Laws of Life*[*] essay contest through my local community foundation along with the Templeton Foundation, set up by legendary investor the late Sir John Templeton. Sir John founded the Templeton Funds in the 1950s. When he retired in the early 1990s, his flagship Templeton Growth Fund had the best 40-year track record in the business and he was widely respected for his value approach to investing. Sir John was a philosopher and philanthropist, as well as a prolific author in both the investment and personal development areas.

At that point, I had spent about 10 years in the investment business and Sir John Templeton had become one of my idols for his kind and generous nature, as well as his investment acumen. While working on the *Laws of Life* project, my contact at the Templeton Foundation learned about my investment background and that I was active in a church that Sir John supported. The contact person commented that with all the things we had in common Sir John would probably like to meet me. A few weeks later, here comes a handwritten note from Sir

---

[*] The Laws of Life Essay Contest is a character-themed essay competition for students, originally created by Sir John Templeton in 1987 in Winchester, Tennessee. The contest challenges young people to discover through reflection and writing what matters most to them in their own lives and the principles they believe should guide their behavior and choices.

John inviting me to visit him at his home in Nassau, Bahamas, if I should ever be in the area.

The next year I made the trip to Nassau and was able to spend a private hour with Sir John Templeton. At that time, it was the highlight of my career. However, I don't tell this story merely to stroke my ego, I want to relate a great moment of clarity that sprung out of this adventure.

A few weeks after coming back from the Bahamas, I was walking by the office TV that ran the financial news station all day. A talking head was saying that investors should "buy an investment and hold it forever just like investment greats Peter Lynch and Sir John Templeton say to do." I stopped in my tracks and thought, *that is not what Sir John would say.* One of Sir John's flagship quotes was *"buy a good bargain and hold it until you find a better bargain."* That is very different than buy-and-hold forever, and in fact, Sir John's portfolios had a completely new set of investments every three to five years on average.

I knew that Peter Lynch had built the Fidelity Magellan Fund into the largest mutual fund in existence during the 1970s and 80s, but I had never looked at how often he traded. I was astounded to see that his average holding period for a stock during his 18-year tenure at Magellan was less than a year. One year, his average holding period was four months! And someone on TV was holding him up as an icon of buy-and-hold.

As I pondered this obvious disconnect between the facts and what the news was telling me, I realized that I was seeing the face of the Wall Street propaganda machine. At that moment, the course of my investment career was changed for the better.

I rarely listen to the financial news because so much of it is misinformation, whether it is about specific investments or general investment advice. Most of it is designed to manipulate you into doing what will serve the interests of Wall Street - usually at your expense. The inducements are familiar: lower taxes, lower expenses, less effort and returns that may beat the other styles of investing – if you look at the time periods they want you to see. Often, influenced by these myths, many investors stay in the stock market regardless of the risks or the ultimate cost to themselves or their families.

Personally, I like to make my decisions based on facts that can't be spun by Wall Street.

Even well-regarded sources have their biases which affect recommendations. There is a saying in the automotive industry that no car has ever been named Motor Trend's Car of the Year that had not first been advertised in their magazine. The same can be said for the financial services industry.

Popular consumer-oriented financial magazines often recommend only no-load mutual funds to their readers. It is not because no-load funds always perform better than load funds, because they don't. The simple explanation is that no-load funds tend to be the only funds that advertise in their magazine. That also has a simple explanation. Commissioned funds direct marketing dollars to brokers, advisers and planners who are paid on commission. No-load funds market direct to the customer because there is no commission incentive for financial professionals. So, what seems like a sweeping validation of the use of no-load funds is not at all what it seems, and should be looked at closely.

Ever since that day, when I saw Sir John Templeton misquoted so badly, I have had a cynical eye when it comes to news and you should too. When the person giving advice on TV is affiliated with a pension fund, mutual fund, or hedge fund, you can be assured that their allegiance is to their shareholders, not you. When one says, "We really like XYZ stock" it does not mean they are buying XYZ. If they were it would work against their shareholders to tell you they were buying and have you bid against the fund for shares of XYZ. They have a fiduciary duty to place the interests of their shareholders above all else, including you.

So, when you hear "We really like XYZ and have built it into one of our largest holdings," that is the fund telling the world to buy, so they can sell off some of their large holdings without driving the market down with the huge volumes of sales that accompany these multi-billion-dollar funds.

The takeaway insight from this is that almost all the information you get from these sources will be telling you to do the exact opposite of what would be good for you. Wall Street loves for you to have the downside of an investment so they can profit off you.

PERFECTLY FLAWED SOLUTIONS

In 1992, I had some new, cutting-edge software that recommended allocations of investor money based upon the client's answers to a risk questionnaire and historic investment returns in 50 or so asset classes. This software was based upon a Nobel Prize winning theory called Modern Portfolio Theory (MPT), which ironically was developed in 1960, so it was hardly modern. MPT said that for any level of risk one wanted to take there was a combination of investments that would have produced the greatest return. This new software created lists of recommended investments with percentage allocation, pie charts and a complete investment package. It was absolutely the best sales aide I had ever seen because computers were then seen as some new guru that was all-seeing and all-knowing. When the computer said to invest like this, investors did so without questions.

When I went to conferences, I noticed that other advisers had discovered the sales power of a pie chart and were beginning to use the same kind of software.

One of the issues that slowly began nagging at me as other advisers began to embrace MPT allocation software is that almost all my clients' risk tolerances ended up being in the 4-6 range on a scale of 1-10. Few were 1-2 or 9-10. The 1s and 2s were off buying CDs and the 9s and 10s were playing options, commodities, and speculative stocks. My 4, 5 and 6 clients all ended up getting similar investment recommendations, just in differing amounts depending if they were a 4, 5 or 6.

What bothered me was that if all the other advisers were seeing the same risk tolerances among their clients and using the same kind of software, the vast majority of clients nationwide were being invested in the same way as mine were.

One thing I had learned in the business was that when everyone begins to do the same thing, no one makes any money at it. When the talking head on TV misrepresented what Sir John Templeton and Peter Lynch did to be successful, I had this image of clients all over the country being led like lemmings toward a financial cliff.

Another chilling revelation came when I realized that clients' answers to risk tolerance questions often changed depending upon the market environment when they completed the questionnaire. During bull markets, everyone wants to take risk. The feeling of loss is not in their experience, so they don't equate risk to losing, they equate risk to making money. After a few quarterly statements showing losses, however, that sinking feeling in one's gut gives risk a different meaning.

Even though they could not articulate the desire, clients wanted portfolios that would change with the markets. They wanted to take risk when it was paying off, but also wanted capital preservation when markets were declining. The most common question I got in up markets was "Are we keeping up with the market?" In declining markets, the very same clients might say, "I could have done better than that with a CD!" Most investors didn't know how to put it into words, but they wanted to earn stock market returns in bull markets and CD-like returns in bear markets. Wall Street's buy-and-hold mantra only addresses one half of investors' goals, conveniently ignoring the desire to avoid losses.

I realized that I needed to make sure my clients had the ability to move their money out of harm's way to keep them from being in the herd of lemmings when that cliff appeared. Since the one thing we can count on in life is that things will change, my business became one that uses investments that can adapt to changes in the markets.

That ah-ha moment long ago, when I saw Sir John Templeton misquoted so badly, changed me from an ordinary financial planner/ adviser to one of a rare breed who knows that to serve clients well, I need to have portfolios that do what Wall Street does, not what Wall Street says. Now, although most of my holding periods are measured in months and years, all my investments are planned to change when the market environment changes and to do so on short notice as changes become evident.

STRUCTURAL PROBLEMS IN THE FINANCIAL SERVICES INDUSTRY

" . . . the average client of a brokerage firm is a little like the grunt soldiers on the front lines who may end up being wounded or killed, sacrificing themselves for the good of the generals behind the lines and the citizenry back home."

Will Hepburn

One of the most frequent requests that advisers get from new clients is, "You'll watch my investments for me, won't you?" I'm guessing that you, too, have asked this or a similar question of your advisers. And I would also guess that the adviser almost always says, "Sure! Of course! You bet!" But do they really act proactively on your behalf? Probably not, because the simple fact is they can't.

When you ask for this type of service you are voicing an expectation that your adviser will either move your money out of harm's way if a market decline is underway, or at least call you to suggest a move whenever preserving your investment capital seems wise. Despite your expectations of proactive work from your adviser, this just cannot happen due to structural impediments in the industry as a whole, and it leads to frequent disappointments in the level of service you receive.

How can there be structural impediments to serving clients? Let me explain.

The vast majority of financial advisers are licensed through FINRA, the Financial Industry Regulatory Authority. If you are familiar with a national investment house, chances are that it and its representatives are licensed through FINRA because FINRA regulates every Broker/Dealer in the country.

The term Broker/Dealer is an obscure one, so it could use some explaining. Brokers are firms that execute transactions of securities owned by others for a commission. Dealers, on the other hand, sell securities that they own in their own inventory and make profits by marking up the price of their securities like any retail store that buys at a wholesale price and sells higher to you.

FINRA has the most restrictive regulations in the industry because the majority of complaints that get filed are against Broker/Dealer firms. The firms' investment representatives are not required to act in your best interest as a fiduciary, but can put the firm's interest or their own interest above yours. This creates a lot of problems as you might expect.

The structural impediments in the industry are caused by the well intentioned regulatory efforts to reduce abuse of you and your money. Unfortunately, the baby can often get thrown out with the bath water.

When you ask your broker/adviser "You will watch my investment, won't you?" intending for them to move your money out of harm's way if a decline is happening, the regulatory environment actually restricts what they can do for you. If the broker earned a commission on your first investment, they aren't allowed to earn another commission if they move your money into a safe harbor without being suspected of "churning" investments just to rack up commissions for themselves. For this reason, commissioned brokers are not allowed to have the discretion to move your money without your specific approval. The appearance of churning raises a red flag for the FINRA auditors, so Broker/Dealers have rules to prevent advisers from doing it. For this reason, few advisers can actually move your money into a safe harbor for you, regardless of what you want.

If, to avoid churning allegations, the adviser does try to move you into a non-commissioned investment such as a different mutual fund in the same family, they will need to speak with you to get your approval before doing the trade. Keep in mind they will earn nothing for this work. And, if they have hundreds of clients it can take a long time to call and service each of them. If you think you are special enough to warrant this kind of attention from your adviser for free, do you really think they will spend the time it takes to do the same for their hundreds of other clients, all for nothing? Will your adviser take on the liability of possibly being wrong in the move recommended and having you complain or demand compensation for losses, all for nothing? Would his firm let him do the work and take the risk, all for nothing? Not hardly. And for this reason, most firms discourage this kind of activity by their representatives.

The retail broker/adviser/planner usually does not have the software or administrative support to buy or sell for groups of clients at one time. The Broker/Dealers they work for require them to do transactions for one client at a time, so the Broker/Dealer has an opportunity to supervise the transaction for appropriateness.

While the brokerage firms can and do actively trade their own portfolios, as a retail client, you face a regulatory structure that keeps you from doing much more than buy an investment and hope it works out. This is the structural impediment that the average client is hampered by without ever knowing why or how.

In fairness to the brokerage community, if everyone were to sell during a market decline the proactive management of investments that I advocate would stop working because the market could be driven to zero as a wave of sellers hit the market. October 19, 1987 showed what could happen when a big imbalance of sellers hits a market. The Dow Jones Industrial Average dropped 23% in just one day!

So, these restrictions do provide some needed equilibrium to the markets. This also creates a significant market niche in which some of us without commission-based conflicts of interest can proactively trade without onerous regulatory restrictions. I am a longtime advocate of proactive investment management and years ago I would get frustrated with the well-polished PR push by Wall Street that continually tells investors to just buy-and-hold while Wall Street does the exact opposite with their own money. Then I realized that we can't all be active in our accounts without destroying the market we all depend on. Now I just smile and remind myself that I and a handful of other managers have the proactive investment management space all to ourselves for a while longer.

Unfortunately, the average client of a brokerage firm is a little like the grunt soldier on the front lines during a battle, who may end up being wounded or killed, sacrificing themselves for the good of the generals behind the lines and the citizenry back home. Hopefully your FINRA licensed investment representative disclosed that to you when you made your investments.

FINDING THE RIGHT FINANCIAL ADVICE

Clearly, buying investments based upon past performance ratings does not work, yet this is the way most investments are sold. So, how do investors protect themselves from well-intentioned but wrong advice?

It helps to start with understanding the financial markets, how Wall Street works, and the propaganda and obstacles individual investors face, as well as how using proactive investment approaches change the investment paradigm. That is a key point of this book, so keep reading.

If you opt to work with an investment adviser or follow investment newsletters, I would suggest you always look for an adviser who has been through several up and down market cycles, and importantly, had his clients/recommendations survive the down market. Skip advisers whose performance is based on post- 2009 years. That was a different world for investors with very smooth sailing through most of the period. It may be a long time before we see another stock market run like that. Find out how the adviser did during the two bear markets of 2000-03 and 2007-09. Ask to see a track record of all the recommendations they made just before that time and how the adviser managed those recommendations during decline. A true money manager keeps this kind of data. A salesman will not!

David Moenning, then with TopStockPortfiolios.com, wrote an article published (ironically) on Morningstar.com that reported on the 2010 Inside ETF (Exchanges Traded Funds) conference in Hollywood, FL, where my friend and past president of the National Association of Active Investment Managers, Ian Naismith, was addressing over 400 financial advisers. Naismith asked the group how many used technical analysis (charts and graphs) or were proactive managers. "At least 75% raised their hands," the article stated. Then he asked how many had been doing it for more than three years (before the 2008 bear market) and half the hands lowered. When he asked how many had been using these methods for 10 years or longer, only a few hands remained up.

What this means to investors is that you will be running into more and more advisers who claim to be proactive managers but have little experience and may never have ridden a full market cycle up and down.

Few managers can handle both kinds of markets. The ones who can are a rare and valuable commodity.

There is no substitute for experience when managing money. If you don't have it, hire someone who does. Don't be fooled, however, into thinking that quoting from someone else's newsletter or website equates to knowing what they are doing. Look for someone who has systems in place and doesn't just fly by the seat of their pants.

It has been said that a wise man learns from his mistakes, but I have found it a lot less expensive to let someone else make the mistakes and learn from them. This is why finding an experienced investment adviser is vitally important to your financial safety.

As we recognize when we grow older, experience can provide tremendous insights that beginners just won't have. This is true for investing as well as life in general.

When you hire a money manager you are buying their experience. Buying a lot of it usually doesn't cost any more than hiring an entry level adviser who doesn't have much experience. By hiring experience, you have a much better chance of having your nest egg emerge intact when the market throws you its next curve.

But, how much experience is enough to really master something?

Technical analysis is the use of charts and graphs to analyze pricing patterns. If it can be said that a picture is worth 1,000 words, then a chart is worth 1,000 numbers. Interpreting the huge volume of data represented in charts is something that one can't become proficient at just by reading a book or taking a class. It takes a lot of experience to get good at it.

In the college classes I taught on *Advanced Investment Analysis* I advised students to look at lots and lots of charts to develop a feel for them. For years, I averaged looking at hundreds of charts per day. To make it doable, I have software that creates short-lists of likely candidates and then automates creation and scrolling through of the charts. This allows me to plow through a huge volume of data in a short amount of time.

Hundreds of charts a day, multiplied by five days a week means 1,000 to 2,000 charts a week for a serious technical analyst. That adds up to 50,000 to 100,000 charts a year. I have been actively managing investments since 1994 and using technical analysis for 20 years. The math tells you that I have looked at somewhere around a million charts in my career – maybe more. Enough that at a glance, I can recognize investments gathering strength and ones losing momentum. That is a serious amount of experience.

As an example of how experience works, let's discuss the great American investment creed of *buy low, sell high.* If you were to take it literally you would never buy something with a high price and only buy investments that were bottoming. Yet, the one trait that the biggest winning investments all share is that they set new high prices as they go up, often as many as 100 times in a year. If you want to seek out the big winners, buying an investment at a new high is one clue. Yet overly simple aphorisms would have you overlooking this important angle.

The stock market has lost 50% of its value twice since the year 2000. A rookie may have a Pollyanna attitude hoping that the worst is now behind us. History, however, strongly suggests that the next 10 years will bring two or three more of these stomach churning declines.

Remember that in investing, "hope" is a four-letter word. When the next crash happens, who do you want advising you on your investments, a seasoned pro who recognizes the problems coming, who has valuable insights and a plan of action, or a financial product salesman with no real track record?

Don't be fooled into settling for a rookie buy-and-hope-it-works-out money manager, or anything close to that. Demand a proactive manager who can be nimble during market declines and has a track record that began before the deep bear markets since 2000 so you can gauge the manager's skill in turbulent markets.

So, to answer the question of "how much experience is enough to master something?" I don't think you can ever get enough. Masters never quit learning.

CHAPTER 4 - POPULAR WALL STREET DELUSIONS

"If Wall Street wants the average investor to buy investments and never sell them, while Wall Street folks are being active traders themselves, and they end up with much of the money because of this, which strategy do you think works the best? Are you beginning to see the face of the Wall Street propaganda machine?"

Will Hepburn

INVESTMENT BANKS

Sorry Virginia, there is no Santa Claus, there is no Easter Bunny and there is no bottomless cash register on Wall Street.

When one sells an investment, cash, referred to as "liquidity" in the markets, must be provided by buyers willing to pay that price. It doesn't matter if you are talking stocks, bonds, real estate or collectibles like coins, each seller must be matched with a buyer before something will happen. No buyer, no sale.

If buyers begin to hesitate before deciding to buy, the imbalance between buyers and sellers can be like a rowboat when people keep moving to one side. At some point, when enough people move, the balance changes and the boat will flip. This is what happened during the stock market crashes of 1929, 1987, 2001 and 2008. All the buyers got so nervous, they decided to just wait and see. Without buyers in the market, sellers were forced to watch as the price they could sell at dropped and dropped and dropped until bargain hunters were finally attracted into the market. The boat flipped onto the side of too many sellers. Trillions of dollars of savings were wiped out in those crashes. Maybe some of that was yours.

Wall Street is made up of hedge, pension and mutual funds and investment bankers who create and provide products (stocks, bonds etc.) to the funds. These folks usually trade in the many billions of dollars a day and are referred to as the "smart money." One reason they appear to be so smart is that they have the size and incentive to manipulate the pools of buyers and sellers to keep the boat from flipping out from under themselves. Usually this is at the expense of individual investors like yourself, called "retail" investors by Wall Street.

Few investors understand that the investment banks make much more of their profits from fees generated by creating new issues of stocks and bonds than with commissions and fees paid by retail customers (you).

As an example, let's say that privately held XYZ company wants to sell stock to raise money and "go public." The Investment Bank, which in this case we shall call Wall Street, creates one billion shares of stock to be sold at $10 per share for a total of $10 billion initial public offering (IPO). XYZ does not want to be in the business of selling stock to retail investors like you and I, so in one transaction, Wall Street gives XYZ company $9.5 billion for the entire block of stock, and XYZ can go about its business of making widgets or whatever.

In our example, Wall Street now has risk because they hold all this stock in their own portfolio. If the price were to go down while Wall Street held the shares, they could lose a lot of money. So, their highest priority becomes moving the newly created shares from their portfolio into investors' hands as quickly as possible. This resale of the stock is often arranged beforehand and the shares are transferred instantly at $10 per share making a tidy $500 million profit for Wall Street in just a few hours, with only a smidgen of risk.

The process I've just described is called "underwriting an issue" and can only be done by investment banks, who along with other huge institutions like hedge funds, mutual funds and pension funds make up much of the Wall Street gang.

$500 million made on a $9.5 billion investment is just over 5.25% profit in a very short time. If you can make 5.25% every day you will have a VERY good year. Heck, do that once a month, your money grows 85% per year. Now you know why I say Wall Street makes much more money underwriting than they do in retail commissions.

Some of our largest investment banks are also well-known brokerage firms:

- JPMorgan Chase.
- Goldman Sachs.
- Bank of America Merrill Lynch.
- Morgan Stanley.
- Citigroup.
- Barclays Investment Bank.
- Credit Suisse.
- Deutsche Bank.

If Wall Street wants to sell their new shares quickly they need a large pool of investors ready to take the other side of the trade – to buy. Wall Street is the "Sell Side" of the business, and they need you to be the buy side. This is why Wall Street puts out many buy recommendations on stocks but very few sell recommendations. Wall Street often needs to unload big blocks of stocks from their own portfolios, and sell recommendations make it harder for them to do that. Can you see the massive conflict of interest?

Often large blocks of stocks (think millions of shares) are sent to the retail investment advisers of these brokerage houses when an institutional customer, perhaps a hedge fund, has issued a sell order. The brokerage firm's motivation is to see the shares moved into retail hands as quickly as possible to reduce the risk of holding them.

When shares like this are offered to you in retail transactions, you don't know what persuasion tools are being used on your financial adviser to get the offering sold. Sometimes an extra commission is offered, or commissions on other securities are cut back until the shares in the block sale have been moved. You really have no way of knowing at the time what the situation actually is.

Wall Street firms are great at preaching buy-and-hold, or hold for the long run, but if you look at how brokerage firms and investment banks trade for their own accounts, it is anything but buy and hold. They are among the most active traders in the market. The term "program trading" was developed for these firms who constantly trade using computers to automatically generate the trades.

So, if Wall Street wants the average investor to buy investments and never sell them while they are being active traders themselves, and Wall Street ends up with much of the money because of this, which strategy do you think works the best? Are you beginning to see the face of the Wall Street propaganda machine?

MUTUAL FUNDS AND MUTUAL FUND MANAGERS

"Put your eggs into fewer baskets and watch those baskets closely."
Andrew Carnegie

Most investors assume that mutual funds are so large and polished that the fund managers have crystal balls and can do no wrong. The public relations arms of these large fund complexes are very good at making you think that too. No fund managers are perfect, however, and none know what the markets will do tomorrow. Markets are just as hard for them to predict as for you or me.

My work within the industry has allowed me to rub shoulders with many fund managers, and I can tell you with certainty that fund managers are people, too. They have fears and insecurities just like anyone else. They often come to conferences after having a bad year, desperate for ideas and insights to turn their fund around since bonuses and even job retention requires certain levels of performance; so, they are motivated by fear.

A herd mentality often crops up among many fund managers since many are given the same performance benchmarks to meet, such as the performance of the S&P 500 index. Any manager who invests differently and chooses wrong runs the risk of lagging his goal or benchmark and losing his job. For this reason, few funds stray from following their benchmarks. Many mutual funds become what I call "closet index funds" because they will only invest in stocks held in their benchmark indexes.

Funds that strictly follow a particular stock index are usually run by unthinking computer programs and as such compete on the basis of low management fees. Some fund companies, wishing to garner fees that can be as much as 10 times higher than index funds, advertise themselves as actively managed to justify the fees. However, if an actively managed fund has a performance benchmark of the S&P 500, and the manager knows that if he underperforms he can be fired, his survival instinct will lead him to invest as closely to the S&P 500 as possible to mimic its performance and not risk his job.

If you look at the mutual fund universe, about 1/3 of funds advertise themselves as true index funds with no real management of the assets beyond rote movements to track the index. Another 1/3 advertise themselves as actively managed funds but have returns that closely follow the returns for their benchmark index because the managers are restricted in the level of management they are allowed to provide by the fund's investment policies. So, for practical purposes, fully 2/3s of all mutual funds act like index funds and you, as the investor, get very little in the way of the management that you expect.

Of the remaining 1/3 of the funds that claim to be actively managed, about half will stay fully invested, but move from one sector to another, such as selling manufacturing stocks and moving that money into utilities or another sector. Staying fully invested in a bear market is like the captain of the Titanic being so sure his ship could survive anything. When the whole market goes down as we see in major bear markets, eventually you go down too.

In my experience, about one in six mutual funds is truly actively managed where a manager can do what he does best, make moves that can outpace markets or protect your principal by getting out of the market completely when the bear is at the door.

Fund managers can also be hampered by requirements that they over-diversify due to fund policy or regulations placed upon funds that claim to be diversified investments. Most fund managers have 10 or 20 really good investment ideas at any one time. If the fund is required to hold 100 or 200 stocks, this means that 9 out of 10 stocks you will own in that fund are not the manager's best picks. In my opinion, the best funds are those whose managers are allowed to concentrate their assets into a small number of stocks. As a proactive investor, I prefer funds that focus their investments like this. As Andrew Carnegie once encouraged investors to do, "Put your eggs into fewer baskets and watch those baskets closely."

Another aspect of herd mentality is due to the location of the major mutual fund complexes, the majority of which are in New York or a short drive away. This means that when companies want to promote their stock to fund managers, almost all of the mutual funds will get the same dog and pony show, and end up with the same information with which to make decisions.

Legendary investor Sir John Templeton credited much of his success to his decision to move his headquarters to St. Petersburg, Florida in the early 1970s. Because few companies made the trip to St. Pete to tout their stock, Templeton managers were forced to do their own research and look for information from sources different from run of the mill fund managers. As a result of this dynamic, Templeton funds' performance began to be consistently far above the average mutual fund.

Most investors misunderstand just what kind of management they will get from a fund manager. If you expect them to get your money out of harm's way when the market begins to head south you will likely be disappointed, as few mutual funds actually do that.

The amount of real managing a fund manager can do is often restricted by prospectus or by fund policy. They are literally handcuffed by their prospectuses to keep them from providing the kind of management most investors expect.

If a prospectus says that 80% of fund assets will be invested in growth stocks, reading between the lines will tell us that if growth experiences a decline similar to what happened in the 2000-2003 bear market, the manager simply cannot move from growth to cash or anything else. The prospectus forbids it. The prospectus says 80%

growth stocks at a minimum. Period. If they do otherwise, they break the law.

Certain fund companies will go beyond the prospectus limitations and stay fully invested as a matter of fund company policy. During the 2000-2003 bear market, which devastated growth stocks, Vanguard's Growth Equity Fund (VGEQX) showed the percentage of equity assets to be above 98% throughout the downturn.

Table 2 - Vanguard Growth Equity Fund investment in equity assets during the 2000-2002 bear market and subsequent years.

VANGUARD GROWTH EQUITY
PORTFOLIO COMPOSITION – % OF ASSETS
DATA UPDATED THROUGH 6-30-2006

YEAR	CASH	STOCKS
As of 6-30-06	1.4%	98.6%
3-Year Average	0.4	99.6
2005	0.7	99.3
2004	0.0	100.0
2003	0.5	99.6
2002	0.7	98.6
2001	0.0	98.7
2000	1.0	93.3

The result of this policy decision was disastrous for the fund's investors as the following chart shows:

Table 3 - Impact on Vanguard Growth Equity Fund returns from high levels of equity assets during the 2000-2002 bear market and subsequent years.

VANGUARD GROWTH EQUITY
PERFORMANCE HISTORY – FISCAL YEAR ENDED SEPTEMBER
DATA UPDATED THROUGH 6-30-2006

	2006	2005	2004	2003	2002	2001	2000
NAV	10.44	10.42	9.66	9.18	6.64	9.64	13.28
Total Return %	0.19	7.88	5.35	38.56	-30.94	-27.41	-23.10
+/- S&P 500	-2.52	2.97	-5.53	9.87	-8.84	-15.52	-14.00

Data from Morningstar

Those 2000-2002 losses for Vanguard Growth Equity compound out to a 66.8% loss. That amount of loss requires an investment to triple in value just to get back to even. How long would it take the fund to triple for its investors? We will never know because Vanguard discontinued the fund. What I can tell you is gains that large take a long, long time for a mutual fund to produce.

Prospectus and policy limitations can provide investors with certainty about what their money is invested in, but that can also be a two-edged sword. If you want the level of management that says it is time to move to a different type of investment, you or your adviser must make that decision because the fund manager won't. In a bear market, the managers of roughly 2/3s of all mutual funds won't be able to do much more for you than rearrange the deck chairs on the Titanic.

In 2001, I spent parts of three days interviewing the managers of the Invesco family of mutual funds. I had a private breakfast one morning with the then manager of the Invesco Telecommunications fund, at that time one of the largest telecom funds in the business. The fund had lost about $500 million (25%) for its investors during the previous year, and at breakfast the manager reminded me of a wide-eyed scared rabbit as he said "This is really a bad decline. We don't see the end of it. We see it going on for another year, perhaps two." I had been looking over his fund's statistics and the fund was still 94% invested in stocks. Being a believer in selling high and buying low, I asked him why he stayed fully invested if he knew things were going to get worse? Shouldn't he be selling stocks and raising cash to be used to buy back in at lower prices?

He looked at me like I had just fallen off the turnip truck and responded, "When people invest in our fund, we assume they want their money in telecom stocks, and we assume if they want to be in cash they will withdraw from the fund."

How many times have you ever had a financial adviser tell you that? I'm guessing never. This is why, when you are in a fund that stays fully invested in any market segment, either you or your adviser must be ready to say when it is time to get out.

The fund managers strictly adhered to their prospectus and investment policy. Invesco Telecom lost another 50% of its value over the next two years creating life-altering losses for investors who did not know when to get out.

Advisers paid on commission are normally prohibited from moving commissioned investments around due to the potential for "churning" – the movement of investments that generate extra commissions for the investment representative. So, investors who expect fully flexible management of assets from either their adviser or their mutual fund are usually disappointed when the market inevitably cycles down and they see formerly good investments take stomach-churning losses.

Some investment managers fill that gap between what clients expect and what mutual funds and traditional financial advisers are able to deliver. They are known as proactive managers and are prepared to move entire portfolios to cash or other safe harbors in times of trouble. If this is what you expect from your manager, you need to ask some very pointed questions about whether your adviser can actually do this for you, because most cannot.

TARGET-DATE FUNDS

"It is absolutely insane to blindly move investors into bond funds as interest rates are creeping up - but this is exactly what Target-Date Funds do."

Will Hepburn

Index mutual funds were all the rage in the 1990's and are becoming so again. Some firms actually promote index funds as "safe" since you should never do worse than the market as a whole. And index funds have broad appeal because they are simple and easily understandable in an industry that is anything but easy and understandable. One investment covers it all for you. That little bit of comfort is a powerful motivator for many investors.

Index funds gained popularity in the 1990s not because they were really that good, but because they had been in sync with the stock market's major trend and looked good for a few years – until the S&P 500, one of the largest stock indexes, lost almost half of its value from

2000-02 and lost half again in 2007-09. The mind has a marvelous capacity to forget pain, however, so investors are once again piling into index funds.

The darling of the industry today is Target-Date Funds, usually a blend of index mutual funds. They are supposed to make saving for retirement easy by offering a pre-mixed portfolio of mutual funds that get more conservative as the years pass. All an investor has to do is select a target retirement date and voilá! An instant retirement portfolio is created for you. One investment covers it all.

No more need to visit that pesky broker. No need to pay a real money manager. And best of all, no more decisions to make. Nirvana for the average investor!

Target-date funds are sometimes called lifestyle funds. You'll know you have one by the year, such as 2030, 2035, 2040 etc., appearing in the fund name. These funds have become very popular because they make investing seem easy and everyone seems to like the softer, easier way of doing things. Target-date mutual funds are the industry's latest attempt at making investing a single, simple decision.

Just tell the fund company when you plan to retire, and as time progresses, the fund manager will gradually adjust your stock/bond investment mix, cutting back on stocks and adding more bonds as you get closer to retirement. This makes sense in a general financial planning manner. An investor should take less risk as the need to access savings gets close and, according to the text books, bonds have less risk than stocks. The problem is that rules of thumb like this are generalizations that often don't work

As you may remember from Investing 101, bond prices fall as interest rates rise and vice-versa. My research tells me that over the next decade or two, bonds are going to be a huge disappointment because interest rates have begun a multi-decade rise, meaning bonds are in for a multi-decade period where they struggle just to break even. Inflation and rising interest rate markets spell big trouble for bonds.

The portfolio changes in target-date funds are fairly mechanical, following a pre-set formula described in fund prospectuses. The fund managers have so very little discretion about how to manage the fund that the term *management* seems so wrong – but I digress. After opening a target-date fund, you don't have to make any further decisions – at least that is how the pitch goes.

Successful investing is anything but simple, and this seductive sales pitch is attractive to the lazy side in each of us. But target-date funds are leading investors on a very dangerous path. In fact, I would not be surprised if target-date funds will be the scandal du jour a few years from now after investors get massive disappointments as target-date funds ignore the realities of the current market. As a professional money manager, I have to tell you that I think it is absolutely insane to blindly move investors into more bond funds as interest rates are creeping up - but this is exactly what target-date funds do - unthinkingly move investors to more and more bonds as time goes on.

Target-date research often compares different target-date fund offerings to show you which fund is best in class. With the looming disaster awaiting target-date fund investors, I liken this kind of research to a discussion about which seat to be in on a plane that is running out of gas.

Morningstar in their 2013 Target Date Research Paper speaks highly of the fact that if turned to income at the investor's age of 65, most target-date funds are not likely to run out of money before age 85; but they say that after that, "results diverge greatly." Uh-huh.

Considering that a retiree at age 65 could stuff money in the mattress, pull out 5% a year and still have the money last until age 85, Morningstar seems to be just putting lipstick on this pig.

Rising stock markets in recent years have helped target-date funds turn in strong returns, but this merely puts a smoke screen around the fact that the bond portion of target-date fund portfolios have under-performed their long-term averages, a trend which is expected to continue as interest rates rise. This combination of falling bond prices as interest rates rise and a formulaic investment plan that keeps moving more of an investor's money into this poorly performing asset class will cause millions of investors to be disappointed by the returns they get from target-date funds, and perhaps not be able to retire as they had hoped.

The long-term total return of the Vanguard Total Bond Market Fund, which follows the Bloomberg Barclays U.S. Aggregate Float Adjusted Index[†], from December 31, 1988 to June 30, 2017 has been 6.46%, with dividends reinvested. These are the kind of returns being factored into projections for the bond portion of most target-date funds. However, between December 31, 2012, when the interest rates began to bottom and bond prices began to peak, and December 29, 2017, the Barclays U.S. Aggregate Float Adjusted Index has produced a total return of only 1.91%, dividends reinvested. (Source: FastTrack) The tide is going out on target-date funds.

When investors expect 6% returns and investments deliver 1/3 of that amount for long periods that is a recipe for a big disappointment. This is the same type of calculation that has so many pension plans in trouble around the country.

When retirement income planning is based upon this type of projection, investors can find themselves reduced to eating dog food as they grow old. They will have run out of money because the largest portion of their target-date portfolios will have been in bonds at a terrible time to be a bond investor.

As the prospectus says, "Past performance does not assure future results." However, past performance is what most investors look at before investing – that and the Siren's song, "Make only one decision and the rest happens automatically."

History strongly suggests that we will experience a prolonged period of generally rising interest rates. We just finished more than 30 years of falling interest rates which pushed bond prices up and up and up. The returns of target-date funds increased with them, but that is changing. Interest rates appear to have bottomed over the past few years, changing the tail wind of rising bond prices into a head wind of falling bond prices that will hold back the returns of target-date funds.

[†] Bloomberg Barclays U.S. Aggregate Float Adjusted Index represents a wide spectrum of public, investment-grade, taxable, fixed-income securities in the United States - including government, corporate, and international dollar-denominated bonds, as well as mortgage-backed and asset-backed securities-all with maturities of more than one year.

Will retirement hopes be dashed like we saw during the stock market crashes in 2002 and 2008 as a growing number of IRA, 401k and retirement plan investors own target-date funds that are destined to disappoint? That possibility is increasing.

Adding more bonds to a portfolio right now is exactly the opposite of what a prudent investor should be doing.

If your mutual funds have a year in the name, such as 2035 or 2040, you need to wake up. You have a target-date fund. Sure, that is an easy way to invest, and there are lots of easy ways to lose money. This is just one. However, the idea is to NOT lose money, and the probability of target-date funds losing money over the next 10, 20 or 30 years is high.

In my opinion target-date funds ignore a basic rule of investing. *There is a time to be invested and a time to be out of the market.* Unthinking, formulaic investing will always run into problems by not being able to adapt to changes in the markets.

Some companies are adding conservative, moderate, and aggressive versions of their target-date funds, but the flaw still exists. They are formula-driven computer programs. There is no one to ask, "Is this a good time to be invested? Or should I be in the safety of a money market fund instead?"

I guess that is why I have lasted more than 30 years in this business. Because when to invest is the question I always start with. What I can say for sure, is right now is not a time to be loading up on long-term bond holdings.

The solution, the only way to protect asset values in these changing market environments such as the bond market is presenting, is proactive management, not a passive formula or indexed approach. The easiest way to make money is to have more money in asset classes that are going up and less money in asset classes that are going down. Target-date funds have it backward!

OVERLY COMPLEX INVESTMENTS

"In my three decades of Wall Street experience, I have not seen any other product as absurdly destructive as retail investments linked to structured products." Louis Straney

Warren Buffett is an investment legend primarily due to his simple approach to investing based partly upon the philosophy, "Never invest in anything you don't understand." For this reason, he has avoided some red-hot technology stocks and he sticks to companies that are easy to understand - predictable cash flow-oriented businesses such as Coca-Cola, See's Candies, railroads, Dairy Queen, etc. Furthermore, Warren Buffett prefers to own two main types of investments - stocks and bonds.

There really are only two types of investments. One is debt - investments you are owed such as bonds, mortgages, annuities, and CDs. The second is equity - investments that you own, such as stocks, real estate, or commodities like gold or silver. Any investment you can name can be grouped into one of these two categories. All other investments are packaged investments that derive their value from the underlying debt or equity investments they are based upon. However, the further you get from the basic stock or bond security, the more layers of fees will be built into the price you will pay compared to plain old stocks and bonds.

Remember that dirty word *derivatives* from the 2008 financial collapse and scandals? Anything beyond the basic stock or bond class of security must derive its value from an underlying debt or equity investment and therefore is really a derivative. Yes, even your mutual fund or indexed annuity is technically a derivative investment. It may not be the wild west of derivatives such as futures, options, or swaps, but mutual funds derive their value from underlying investments, too.

Some derivatives are standardized securities such as futures and options, for which daily pricing is readily available. However, derivatives can also be custom, one-of-a-kind agreements between two parties which are almost impossible to value. These are known as Over-

The-Counter derivatives, meaning that each one is negotiated separately.

Notice that you'll rarely see futures, options, swaps, or OTC derivatives in Berkshire Hathaway's list of top holdings. Warren Buffett avoids expense and complexity in his investments. There are enough investment expenses hiding under the surface of the average investment. Bank, insurance company and investment banking offices are among the biggest and most lavish of buildings. Where do you think the money for those comes from? Uh-huh, you. Your money is the only money in the financial system and layers of fees on complex investments move money from your account to the bank or investment firm. Buffett avoids expense and complexity in his investments. Most investors should too.

Structured notes are Wall Street's derivative du jour for retail investors such as yourself. The insurance industry's version is called indexed annuities. Although at first glance structured notes may appear to be a product that is the answer to your prayers, they are really just one more way Wall Street is going to separate you from your money. ***Investopedia calls these investments "real stinkers", here's why:***

A structured note is an ***IOU*** based upon a derivative that creates the desired exposure to one or more investments, often an investment index. For example, you can have a structured note deriving its performance from the S&P 500 Index, a Treasury bond index or both. The combinations are almost limitless due to the thousands of investments and indexes upon which derivatives can be based. If the investment banks think they can sell it, they will make just about any monetary cocktail you can dream up.

Advantages to investing in structured notes are often stated as diversification, but the underlying assets are probably already in your portfolio somewhere. Elsewhere in this book I talk about effective diversification vs. pointless diversification and using a structured investment for diversification like this seems to be pointless to me.

Some notes advertise an investment return with little or no principal risk. Structured notes have been repackaged into annuities and sold to retail investors — often, senior citizens —as a principal protection tool. They are currently among the most popular products pitched to income-oriented investors.

However, structured products are very complex. Regulators have warned investors that structured notes with principal protection such as in indexed annuities, may have low guarantees, are not risk-free, can tie up money for as long as a decade and come with terms so confusing that many investors cannot understand them. Even with stronger guarantees, if the issuer of the note goes bankrupt, such as Lehmann Brothers did in 2008, the investor may lose much of the money invested.

In his 2011 report on this subject, securities arbitration consultant Louis Straney stated, "In my three decades of Wall Street experience, I have not seen any other product as absurdly destructive as retail investments linked to structured products."

The many layers of fees and commissions really stack the deck against the average investor doing well with structured investments. Structured products pay brokers some of the biggest commissions available anywhere. If you have ever wondered why indexed annuities are the investments most frequently pitched to retirees at free lunch seminars, all you have to do is look at the commission paid on the investment. Some are more than 10%! That, plus the cost of lunch, comes out of your money because you are the only one paying for anything. Keep in mind that there is no such thing as a free lunch.

When you combine the conflict of interest that commission-based investments can create, with the extreme complexity of structured products and indexed annuities, the average investor becomes a sheep ripe for shearing by unscrupulous or unknowing investment salespeople.

Even bank and savings and loan managers were taken by slick salesmen pushing junk bonds in the late 1980s to mid 1990's. These were smart people who were sold a new product they did not fully understand, and the savings industry paid dearly for it. Over 1,000 savings and loan companies were killed off completely by complex investments they thought they understood, but didn't. If it can happen to them it can happen to you.

If you have ever tried to really understand every detail in an Indexed Annuity contract, you have seen just how complex structured notes can be. Warren Buffett doesn't buy these investments. Doesn't that tell you something?

CHAPTER 5 - FINANCIAL MARKET REALITIES

"'Just be patient. Markets always bounce back' is more of Wall Street's snake oil. It sounds good, but often doesn't work before an investor runs out of money, or patience, or both."

Will Hepburn

Like so many Wall Street adages, "Markets always bounce back" does have a kernel of truth in it because there is an upward bias to markets over long periods of time. Yet, if you don't have a 50-100-year time horizon, many of the studies and rules of thumb Wall Street promotes can be very misleading despite their technical accuracy. History is full of periods when markets took years to bounce back and investors would have lost money.

If you are a pension fund with a 100-year time horizon, long-term investing is fine. Most academic studies assume this very, very long-term approach to investing. But is that really right for you? When might you want your money? Five years? When you retire? Maybe you are uncertain about exactly when you'll want your money, you just want the flexibility of knowing your money is available to you at any time.

STOCK MARKET CYCLES

A typical graph of the stock market looks much like the following, tracing the growth of an index over 50-80 years. We call this the mountain chart. It's accurate, but deceptive. It does not represent the experience of anyone who invests at a point on the timeline other than the start.

Figure 3 - Growth of the S&P 500 Index over a 67-year period.

A more accurate way to view market performance is with a logarithmic graph. A logarithmic scale allows you to work with a large range of numbers and more accurately see the overall trend. It also brings into focus the generational cycles that are inherent in all financial markets.

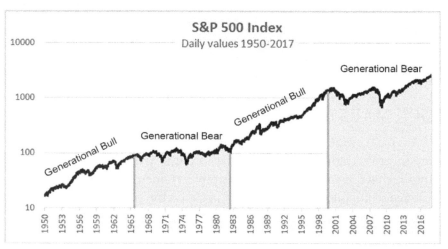

Figure 4 - Logarithmic scale - growth of the S&P 500 Index over a 67-year period

I use the term ***generational bear markets*** to describe long periods of market decline, often 15-20 years which are marked by a series of frequent or deep individual bear markets. The term generational bear market is used not just because the declines last that long, but because they can wipe out a whole generation of investors, or at least sour them so that they never want to consider investing in stocks or bonds again.

If you don't have 100 years to commit your money, then you need to understand what can happen during shorter periods. Here is an illustration that shows the past 215 years of market history. There are many insights in this bit of data, so let's look at what it can tell us.

Table 4 – Stock market cycles encompassing generational bull and bear markets.

Generational Stock Market Cycles
1802 – Present
Average Annual Return, Adjusted for Inflation, 7.00%

From	To	Cycle Leg Length		Annual Returns Bull Leg	Bear Leg	# of Bears	Economy
1802	1815	13	years down		2.7%		
1815	1835	20	years up	10.0%			
1835	1843	8	years down		-0.6%		Deflation
1843	1853	10	years up	13.7%			
1853	1861	8	years down		-0.03%		Inflation
1861	1881	20	years up	12.0%			
1881	1897	16	years down		3.9%		Deflation
1897	1902	5	years up	15.2%			
1902	1921	19	years down		0.0%	6	Inflation
1921	1929	8	years up	25.2%			
1929	1949	20	years down		0.8%	5	Deflation
1949	1966	17	years up	14.0%			
1966	1982	16	years down		-1.4%	4	Inflation
1982	1999	17	years up	14.9%			
2000	??	17	years down?		-1.29%	3	Deflation
Cycle Leg Average Length				13.8	14.5		
Cycle Leg Average Annual Return				15.0%	0.45%		

Source: Robert Powers, PO Box 35, Rapid City MI 49676. Gold-Eagle and Investors FastTrack. Hepburn Capital Management, LLC.

In the 200-odd years represented in the table, stock markets averaged around 7% annually after adjusting for inflation. (If the markets return 10-11% annually in an environment with 3-4% inflation, you end up with around 7% real return.)

During this period, there were seven complete cycles - highlighted to make them easier to identify. We are working on the 8th cycle right now, but the beginning and ending dates can be a little subjective. In the middle of a cycle, turning points can be hard to identify accurately without the benefit of the passage of time.

Each cycle has a down leg (bear markets dominating) and an up leg (bull markets dominating). What differentiates these different up and down cycles is the number and character of the individual bear markets within them. The 1982-1999 period included only two bear markets, 1987 and 1990, which were both short and shallow by historic standards. The 16-year period before that is one that Wall Street likes to ignore because it produced four bear markets, including a whopping 43% loss in 1973-74, a devastating loss to many investors at the time. Applying the math of gains and losses tells us that a 43% loss requires a 75% gain to overcome, just to break even.

The strong cycle in the 1949-1966 period was similar to the 1980s and 90s in that there were only two bear markets, both shorter and shallower than average. The weak period before that was 1929-1949 when there were five individual bear markets, with three of them delivering losses of 47%, 52% and 87%. This was the period of the Great Depression which wiped out a whole generation of savers.

This pattern of long periods of strength followed by long periods of stock market weakness is persistent for over 200 years. The down legs are what I earlier referred to as Generational Bear Markets.

The different cycle legs average close to 14 years. The longest Generational Bears are recent ones with 16 years, 20 years and 19 years respectively. Using these times as a guideline, we might look at the current market to try to discern where we are in the cycle.

WHERE IS THE S&P 500 TODAY?

Clearly, we have experienced a Generational Bear, with a 52% decline and a 56% decline in the S&P 500 since the year 2000. Arguably, there have been two smaller declines in 2011 and 2015-16 that could be considered bear markets if we don't get overly strict about the definition of a bear market. The 2011 decline did not quite get under the 20% loss threshold looking at closing prices only. However, there was a point in 2011 when the S&P 500 Index dipped 21.58% before closing higher that day, just above the -20% level. We can debate if that was really a bear market, but to market participants in 2011 it felt like one.

The 2015-16 bear market was a documented bear in just about all other countries, but only came close in the U.S. So, was 2015-2016 a bear market? Considering that the U.S. market represents only 36% of the global market capitalization, probably, but some U.S. academics would argue about that. I'll let you decide. All of this puts the total number of bear markets between two and four depending upon your reasoning.

The difficulty in counting the number of individual bear markets in the current Generational Bear is further compounded by when one begins. Some would argue that the 2000-2003 bear market was just a cyclical downturn in the technology markets caused by the tech overbuild in anticipation of Y2K. In fact, value stocks did very well with many value funds producing net gains in the 2000-2003 period.

Bear markets are generally broad-based declines. To have gains in large portions of a stock market suggests that the cyclical decline theory has merit. The same people would argue that the true generational market change began in 2007 when banks began failing and the entire financial landscape was affected.

So, determining when this Generational Bear will be over depends on when one starts counting - 2000 or 2007? Adding the 16- to 20-year recent cycle lengths to these two dates tells us that the Generational Bear should be over between 2016 and 2027 – if you believe the problems we are facing are no worse than average.

The data in our chart also suggests that we should expect from four to six individual bear markets before the Generational Bear rolls over and bull market domination begins. Everyone can agree that we have had one bear market, the whopper in 2007-2009. But how confident can we be that the Generational Bear began in 2000, or that 2011 and 2015-16 were bear markets that should be counted? If we count all the disputed bear markets, we would have had four of them since 2000. Is this the kind of Generational Bear that deserves the minimum number of individual bears or will we have more bear markets before we return to the smooth sailing of the 1980-90s, a Generational Bull Market?

We cannot dismiss the possibility that we are still in a Generational Bear Market and have one or more individual bear markets coming, perhaps one with devastating financial impact such as we have seen twice since the year 2000.

Since there are only opinions with which to answer these questions, I guess it comes down to how lucky do you feel?

BONDS ARE CYCLICAL AS WELL

The Foundation for the Study of Cycles (*foundationforthestudyofcycles.org*) has compiled the following chart showing yields of high-grade corporate bonds going back 265 years.

Current bond indexes such as *Moody's Aaa* Corporate Bond only began 100 years or so ago, so data from earlier periods has been pieced together from historical documents. For this reason, it may be a bit more subjective since the data prior to 1919 is not easily verifiable. Other similar works of bond history show different values; however, all deliver a compelling picture of interest rate trends over long periods.

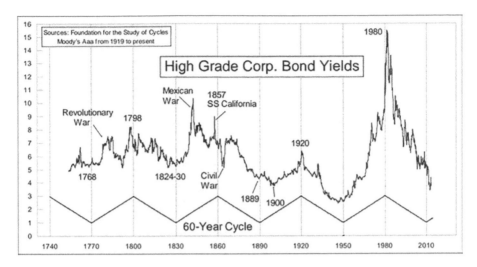

Figure 5 - Cyclical pattern of high-grade corporate bond yields dating back to 1768 in the data set.

There are important bottoms for interest rates, which can be seen near the years 1770, 1830, 1890, and 1950. Each of these bottoms arrives approximately 60 years after the prior one. The next major bottom for interest rates was ideally due in 2012; however, long cycles like this are rarely so punctual. With the Federal Reserve Bank putting its thumb on the scale through various quantitative easing (QE) efforts, which really amount to printing money to keep interest rates down, it is no wonder that the interest rate cycle low expected in 2010 has come a few years later than normal.

The real point is that after the long period of declining rates is finished, which appears to have bottomed in the summer of 2016, a long period of rising rates is due to complete the cycle.

The Fed first announced that it would taper off its QE efforts in 2014, however, central banks in Europe and Japan were still flooding the world with their currencies. Since both European bonds and Japanese bonds had negative yields due to their central bank actions, many Euros and Yen found their way to the U.S. bond markets, which sported better yields. In 2016, Europe appeared to be coming out if its long recession and the European central banks began to reduce their

QE efforts also. This pushed the cycle low to 2016, and rates appear to have bottomed for real in the summer of 2016.

If we are correct in our assumption that the 2016 low in interest rates was the cycle low, then this suggests we have approximately 30 years of generally rising rates ahead.

HOW HIGH CAN INTEREST RATES GO?

How high can interest rates go during their 30-year rise? Using 10-year Treasury bonds as a proxy for the bond market, their historic average yield since 1962 is 6.26% (Source: Yahoo Finance). However, when markets cycle, they normally don't snap back to average. They go from absurdly low to absurdly high, which is what creates the long-term average.

The following table shows what is likely to happen to Treasury bonds in a rising interest rate environment.

Table 5 - Impact of a rising interest rate environment on U.S. Treasury bonds.

3% Treasury Bond Values

Priced to Yield	10-Year Maturity	20-Year Maturity
3%	$ 100.00	$ 100.00
4%	$ 88.03	$ 80.35
5%	$ 84.41	$ 74.90
6%	$ 77.68	$ 65.33
7%	$ 71.58	$ 57.29
8%	$ 66.02	$ 50.52
9%	$ 60.98	$ 44.80
10%	$ 56.38	$ 39.94

This cycle expectation just happens to coincide with the arrival of Baby Boomers at an age when traditional investment advice is telling them they should load up on bonds to be safe in retirement. As they have many times in the past, Wall Street is encouraging investors to all pile into another financial asset, this time it is bonds, at precisely the wrong time, just like they did with tech stocks in 1999 and housing and mortgage stocks in 2005-06.

The following chapters will help you decide how to navigate the iceberg infested waters of the financial markets and make this decision with an investing confidence you may have never had before.

CHAPTER 6 – THE IMPORTANCE OF CAPITAL PRESERVATION

"Just like a passenger on a cruise boat enjoys smoother seas rather than rough seas, you probably like smoother returns while your money is working for you."

Will Hepburn

As dark as the stock market may seem from time to time, bear markets always reach a bottom eventually and a tremendous profit opportunity presents itself as markets rebound off the bottom.

Some investors think that capital preservation means retreating to CDs the day before the market news becomes scary. This is not very realistic since we never know when the market is going to go down or if it will bounce at the end of a decline until those moves are under way and losses or gains have already occurred. Even professional money managers don't have psychic abilities, but they do have systems that tell them how to recognize what is currently happening and the appropriate action to take.

When clients ask me "When will this (bear or bull market) be over?" I reply that I can't say for sure because I don't have a crystal ball, but I am confident that by keeping my finger on the pulse of the market I will be able to recognize a market turn when it happens and adjust to it.

In market downturns, the idea is to preserve your capital so when the market does turn around you will have as much of your money as possible to invest in the good times that inevitably follow. At least you'll have more money to work with than a buy-and-hope-it-works-out investor who rides the decline all the way down.

Capital preservation is the single most important thing in keeping you in the top tier of all investors. Let me explain. I'll keep the math simple.

MATHEMATICS OF LOSSES AND GAINS

It is much easier to lose money than it is to make money. This is not voodoo economics, it is the math of gains and losses.

Table 6 – It is much harder to make money than it is to lose money because every time you lose money you have a smaller base from which to rebuild.

Math of Losing

If the decline is:		What it takes to break even:
-10%	→	+11%
-33%	→	+50%
-50%	→	+100%
-75%	→	+300%
-90%	→	+900%

Defense wins!

If you start with $1 and lose half, you have only 50¢ left. If you want to get back to breakeven you must earn 50¢, but you only have 50¢ to do it with. To earn 50¢ on 50¢ takes a 100% gain. So, a 50% loss needs a 100% gain to recover.

In a more real-life example, if the average investor loses half of their money, as has happened twice in the past 20 years, their $500,000 account becomes $250,000. When the rebound begins and the market gains 50%, their gain is only $125,000, not enough to get them back to the original investment. A 50% gain only gets them halfway back to their original investment and a current account value of $375,000. It takes a 100% gain to break even after a 50% loss.

Capital preservation does not have to be perfect to be effective. An account can show small losses and still out-perform the stock market in the long run, as long as losses are smaller than the market as a whole. If one minimizes losses to 10% in a bear market and can start re-investing after the rebound with 90% capital still intact that is a tremendous advantage over those who lose half of their money and have to start over with only 50% of their capital left. A 50% gain on 90% of the original $500,000 would put our hypothetical investor at 135% of his original investment or $675,000 in this example – way ahead of a traditional, buy-and-hope-it-works-out investor.

Even if a proactive approach to investing misses the beginning of the rebound, the proactive investor still has a tremendous advantage over most investors.

As Richard Russell, the late writer of the Dow Theory Letters once said of bear markets, *"Everyone will lose something. Even CD owners lose purchasing power. The winners will be the ones who lose the least."*

And that is the real rationale behind capital preservation.

If I were to ask you which asset class did the best since the year 2000 started, what would you guess? The stock market? Nope. It was high-yield bonds, commonly called junk bonds. From December 31, 1999 to December 29, 2017, the total return of the S&P 500 was 5.37% and the average total return of all junk bond funds was 6.16% for the same period. (Source: FastTrack)

How can this be? The math of gains and losses kicked in when the S&P 500 dropped 52% between 2000-03 and then again when it lost another 56% in the 2007-09 bear market. Junk bonds only dropped 10% and 33% in those same time periods giving them a big math-of-losing advantage. Their much lower volatility compared to stocks really made junk bonds the superior investment since Y2K.

LOWER VOLATILITY IS THE INVESTOR'S FRIEND

An example I use in my classes is to have students choose between two investments, Fund A and Fund B. Fund A returns a very boring 6% every year, and Fund B occasionally hits it out of the park, but occasionally incurred some modest losses. Which would you choose?

Table 7 - Comparison of a low-volatility and high-volatility fund.

Year	Fund A	Fund B
1	6%	15%
2	6%	-10%
3	6%	35%
4	6%	20%
5	6%	-9%
6	6%	4%
7	6%	-8%
8	6%	14%
9	6%	1%
10	6%	4%
11	6%	12%
12	6%	3%

Both funds actually earned the same amount, doubling their money in the 12-year period. The difference is that Fund A experienced much lower volatility and lower demonstrated risk.

There are many ways to look at risk and gauge its effects. There is something called risk-adjusted return, but rather than bore you with the details of the math, let me give you an example of how it works. If you were to invest $100,000 with me on Friday, and on Monday I tell you that I doubled your money over the weekend, you would probably be thrilled. However, how would you feel if I told you that I doubled your money by rolling the dice in Las Vegas all weekend? There would have been a significant chance that you could have also lost everything in one weekend and you probably would not have allowed your money to be exposed to that level of risk, given the choice. This is the idea behind a risk-adjusted return calculation.

Albert Einstein was rumored to have said that *"the most powerful force in the world is compounding."* The idea of constant compounding works both ways, for both gains and losses, and wise investors use this knowledge during investment selection and avoid investments that can compound negatively.

Over the years, I have developed a *Quality of Trend Analysis* that I use to help me select investments for my clients. I am interested not just in getting the highest investment returns but getting the best return possible with the least risk. I want the lowest dips along the way to a respectable return, so if my client looks at their account after seeing scary headlines about the stock market, their peace of mind won't take a hit.

The only thing money is good for is not having to worry about money, and if big swings in your investment values give you a sinking feeling in the pit of your stomach, you should consider moving to something with lower volatility.

At the risk of getting over technical here, there is a statistic that measures how wildly the price of an investment fluctuates along the path to creating its average return. For the math-oriented, this is called standard deviation of returns, although knowing that term is not important. No one really cares how high the waves go, in fact upside volatility is normally cheered by investors. Downside volatility, however, is another thing altogether. Investors are much more sensitive to investments going down than to those going up. Have you ever noticed that about yourself?

There is a measure of downside volatility that ignores the up cycles and focuses only on the downward moves compared to the average return. This indicator is called, appropriately enough, the Ulcer Index.

Dividing the Ulcer Index by the investment return gives an indicator called the Ulcer Performance Index – how much performance does one get for each ulcer with this investment. UPI, as it is called, is a very useful investment tool and an integral part of my *Quality of Trend Analysis*. Some charting programs will calculate UPI for you, by the way.

Just like a passenger on a cruise boat enjoys smoother seas rather than rough seas, you probably like smoother rides while your money is working for you. Rather than just looking at what investments have returned, also look at how they get that rate of return and seek investments that will give you a smoother ride. You may be able to stay in the smoother investment longer without running into losses large enough that they make you want to sell.

No amount of money is worth worrying about, and you should build that factor into your investment selection.

CHAPTER 7 – CYCLES AND THEIR IMPACT ON YOUR INVESTMENTS

"Cycles are an investing reality. Not just shares – but also bonds, property, infrastructure, term deposits, whatever. They all go through cyclical phases of good times and bad, which are driven by the combination of fundamental economic and financial developments invariably magnified by investor behavior."

Shane Oliver

Investing is about dealing with reality: seeing it, recognizing it for what it is, and acting on it in a way that you can profit from. Successful investors know this and have systems for dealing with the realities of the market place. Foremost among those realities are market cycles, those inevitable, never-ending series of ups and downs that stocks, funds and even entire markets go through.

The number one reason why bad things happen to good investments is that many investors ignore the devastating power of market cycles. They blindly follow the clichés, rules of thumbs and formulas that Wall Street generates without looking critically at their personal situation to be sure the cliché of the day is really working for them. Remember, Wall Street loves to get you moving in a direction that will help them, not you.

It took the technology-heavy Nasdaq Index over 15 years to recover after its cycle turned down and posted an -89% decline in 2000-03. Many retirement plans were delayed or dashed completely for investors who had money in technology back then. Cycles that turn down can be very powerful and are something to be respected, perhaps even feared.

One big reality that Wall Street repeatedly glosses over is that markets are cyclical. Yes, they go up, but they are certain to go down as well. Business cycles can evolve over many years. In one phase, the business cycle will favor stock investing over bonds or commodities, and in other phases favor bonds or commodities over stocks. Product cycles can greatly affect a company's fortune. Consider the expiring patent of a blockbuster drug, the wave of 3D printing technology that is affecting entire industries, or the rising price of energy that will spur a wave of new energy conservation technology.

These cycles affect companies, industries, and entire markets. Even good investments cannot escape the reality of investment cycles. In bear markets, consumers begin to see their savings shrink and change their normal spending patterns, buying fewer vacations, houses, and new cars. Since 70% of our economy is based upon consumer spending, those industries enter a declining phase of their cycle. Companies that keep doing a steady business regardless of economic conditions, such as utilities, beer brewers or makers of consumer goods like toilet paper, will do well during bear markets, but will languish when the public's focus returns to vacations, cars, and new houses.

Passively holding stocks makes you powerless to resist a decline when the cycles turn down, as they inevitably will. Wall Street's advice to buy an index fund and passively let the market work for you may catch a few up cycles but will also keep you invested during the long bear market declines that typically follow, causing the value of your savings to fluctuate wildly over time. Is that really what you want as an investor? Is that what Warren Buffett would do?

Like good companies, good funds that stay fully invested during market declines will also be brought down by cycles they cannot resist due to a decision of fund management to stay fully invested regardless of market conditions. Does your fund or ETF stay fully invested through thick or thin? Wise investors know that there are good times to be invested and there are good times to be sitting in cash. Few ETFs or mutual funds are capable of *Adapting to Changing Markets*®. If you own this type of fund or ETF, you or your financial adviser need to make the decision when it is time to move to cash, because most funds won't do it for you.

When market cycles begin to assert themselves, they often affect entire markets, such as the world saw during the financial crisis of 2007-09. As the following chart shows, when one stock market goes down there is often no place for a stock investor to hide because all segments of the stock market go down at the same time.

It did not matter if you were in a large company or small company index, foreign or domestic, in 2008-09 all sectors of the stock market declined at the same time. Diversifying among these stock categories did not help investors in 2008. They merely lost money in more places.

Diversification Fails When You Need It Most

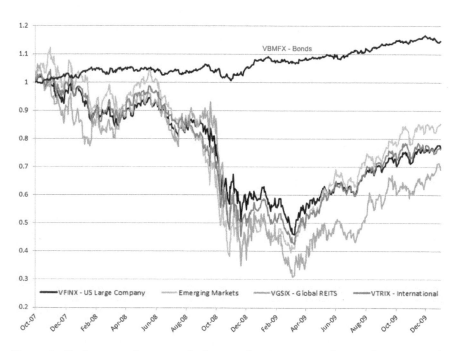

Figure 6 - In down markets, correlations tend to increase and asset classes move in the same direction.

October 2007 – December 2009

RECOGNIZING CYCLES IS THE START TO SUCCESSFUL INVESTING

Investors who can recognize and ride these waves can do much better than the average returns of an index. By reacting when up cycles are weakening, they can sidestep those pesky bear market declines that can set retirement plans back by five or ten years.

Investing can be a very simple if you stop listening to the Wall Street propaganda machine and just move your money out of harm's way during declines. Sometimes the only solution is to just get out of a market that is in decline, and sit in cash, bonds, or something else that is not going down.

A successful investment approach recognizes that you absolutely must have a plan to react to changing market conditions. In 2001, during the bear markets caused by the 2000-03 tech wreck, my strategies that were *Adapting to Changing Markets*® were providing such superior results for my clients that I trademarked the term and have been using both the term and the investment style ever since.

Unfortunately, the average investor is often not confident enough in their ability to recognize what is really happening around them in the markets or to see cycles change amid the blizzard of confusing financial news. Frequently, they are drawn in by the Siren's Song of simple explanations and the spin on events by the Wall Street propaganda machine. Media explanations can make even a clear day on Wall Street seem pretty foggy. However, it doesn't have to be that way.

The kind of systems investors need can be likened to the instruments pilots have to tell them which way is up when flying in clouds. Simple systems, like recognizing that you are losing money and that something needs to change, can allow your savings to go around storms rather than through them.

I was pleased recently to read a news article that critical thinking is emerging as a course of study in elementary schools to help students identify "fake news" in media. Wall Street is not alone in generating fake news poop-poohing the damage done to unaware investors by market cycles. PT Barnum recognized that there was a sucker born each minute, and politicians, industries, scientists, and writers with their own agendas bombard us with scads of fake news every day, playing us for suckers. Rather than real news, most of this stuff is a sales job to get you to think or act in a way that is going to benefit someone else. We can all be better investors if we can begin to see the reality of cycles more clearly and not through the smoke and mirrors of fake news from Wall Street.

Not believing what the media spits out is a good first step. Turn off your TVs. Most of what you see and hear is entertainment at best and propaganda at worst, but it is not news! Learn to trust your eyes and ears. If something you own is losing money, it is losing money! Having Wall Street tell you not to feel too bad, that your losses make total sense in the changing market environment and that you are losing money for all the right reasons does not change the fact that you are losing money in that investment!

Warren Buffett has a simple rule, *to not lose money*. Regardless of what the media suggests, if you recognize that you have an investment that is losing money, it may be time to get rid of that investment! Investing can be that simple. Ignoring Buffett's simple, clear advice can be a life-altering mistake for you.

One of Wall Street's favorite tools is to trot out *truisms* that are then accepted because so many investors are not confident in their own judgment. They rely on what the experts say, not realizing that the experts are manipulating the public for their own benefit. Wall Street will lead you to believe that their rules of thumb should be followed all the time, when the reality is that a good portion of the time they may be a disaster for you personally. When the disaster hits, Wall Street will tell you that these things happen, and you must just be patient. If they really knew so much, maybe they should have advised you to avoid the disaster in the first place!

If you follow the Pied Piper of Wall Street without considering that the media behind the stream of messaging may not be your friend, you are dealing in fantasy not reality. Investors who recognize reality are generally going to be much more successful than investors who float along passively like flotsam on the financial tides.

This is where you, as an individual investor, need to assert control and adapt. Or at least hire an investment adviser who is both willing and capable of adapting for you. I am convinced that when history is written, the cult-like practice of buying and passively holding an index fund will be exposed as one of the great investment flim-flams of history. It might take a few more bear markets to wake investors up to the reality that they need to go back to elementary school for that course in critical thinking that they missed earlier.

As a reader of this book, you may consider yourself exempt from having to repeat that class if you are willing to recognize reality and act on that realization.

CHAPTER 8 - KNOW YOUR INVESTING TEMPERAMENT

"It is always smart to learn from your mistakes, but it's a whole lot cheaper to learn from the mistakes of others instead."

Unknown

That great American philosopher Yogi Berra has a wonderful saying that goes, *"If you don't know where you are going you'll end up somewhere else."* In my college classes, I use this to illustrate the essence of investing.

In 1993, a little old lady was referred to me. Her portfolio held a zero-coupon Treasury bond fund with a 25-year maturity. When I asked her why she owned it, she said she didn't know much about it but her nice neighbor, who was quite the investor, said he owned it, and she figured Treasury bonds sounded good.

The woman didn't know that long-term zero-coupon bonds have the highest market risk of any kind of bond. Sure, the default risk on the bonds is minimal due to all those printing presses at the Treasury Department, but the market risk is many times what a little old lady should be taking, and she didn't have a clue. She didn't know where she was going.

When I explained the risk she faced, her face turned as white as her hair and she asked me to find her something else. Later that year, interest rates rose 30% knocking long-term Treasury prices down hard. The zero-coupon bond mutual fund the woman had owned lost 34% of its value during that same period. (BTTTX, October 15, 1993-November 11, 1994. Source: FastTrack). Fortunately, I had moved her out of that fund before it tanked.

This woman did not have either the knowledge, temperament, or tolerance for that kind of risk, but she was not able to recognize it by herself. She is not alone. Many investors really don't have enough experience to know how to gauge their investment temperament and easily can stumble into retirement-ending mistakes. It is always smart to learn from your mistakes, but it's a whole lot cheaper to learn from the mistakes of others instead.

RISK AND INVESTOR TEMPERAMENT

When prospective clients come in and want a portion of their portfolios in growth stocks, I have learned to ask several questions to better determine their investment temperament and how much they really understand about risk.

If they have plenty of money to retire on, I will ask why they want to take the risk of heavy stock investing. Most just shrug their shoulders and say that's what they have always done. When I ask what would happen to their lifestyle if they doubled their money in the markets, most say nothing would change. After all, how many steaks can one person eat?

When I ask what would happen to their lifestyle if their savings were cut in half by an unforeseeable stock market crash, such as what happened on 9/11, that is when the idea of risk really sets in. Gulp.

Another good way to uncover your investment temperament is to use your actual investment dollars in helping you imagine this series of events. Let's say you have $500,000 to invest in the stock market and your investments follow the S&P 500 Index*.

How will you react if after six months your investment statement shows you lost $100,000 and your account has dropped to $400,000? Will you have a serious meeting with your financial adviser, or a stern phone call with the nice kid at the mutual fund company?

How will you feel if over the next quarter you drop another $50,000 and your account is down to $350,000? Then, over the next quarter you have another $50,000 in losses and your account is down to $300,000. Let that feeling sink in for a minute. You've lost 40% of your savings in one year. Money that took half a lifetime to accumulate. What will you do? Will you just sit tight and do nothing? Do you fire your adviser? Tell the mutual fund company that you could do better than what they have done with a CD and move your money to a bank?

Few clients can withstand that kind of stomach churning roller coaster of emotions as they see a lifetime of savings being eaten up with market losses. After a few quarters of consecutive losses, most investors will choose to fire their adviser or mutual fund company believing evidence of their incompetence is right there in front of them, emblazoned on their statements in red ink.

If you think you can use a buy-and-hold investment approach and hold on through the downturns, know that you will get only average market returns but take the full risk of stock market investing. In the 2000-2003 bear market, the S&P 500 dropped 52%, which would have meant watching your $500,000 portfolio drop to $240,000 over 12 quarters. Would three straight years of losses grind you down and make you abandon your failing stocks or funds?

In the 2007-2009 financial crisis, the S&P 500 dropped 56%. A $500,000 portfolio would potentially fall to $220,000 with this kind of loss - that is if you still had $500,000 left after the 2000-03 crash. The 2007-09 decline only took about 18 months - six quarterly statements - to chronicle the depletion of your retirement savings.

One of the great contradictions of buy-and-hold investing is its simplicity, when in fact so very few can successfully hold through the full up and down of market cycles. Could you watch your portfolio suffer significant declines in bear markets with little guarantee when or if it will recover? If so, you might be cut out for being a buy-and-hold investor. There are good rewards in the up markets, but you need to really understand your investment temperament, or you might get caught in the Average Investor's Curve.

RIDING OUT THE AVERAGE INVESTOR'S CURVE

The average investor, when faced with an investment decision is diligent about this task. They will read news on investments or do Internet searches to know what is working and what is not, and they may talk to friends about how they are making money. Then they may get a prospectus and read up on the fund, its fees and expenses, etc. After doing all this research, they will finally buy the investment.

The problem with this approach is it focuses one's attention simply on what has been going up recently. Due to the relentless nature of market cycles, what has been going up will eventually start going down. The longer you research, and the longer the history of rising prices the investment shows, the closer to the down cycle you will be.

So, let us assume you are an investor with $$$ cash to invest. You do research and invest, and for a while things are working fine and the price goes up. You smile. Then the market stops going up, but you think, "I'm OK, I have a profit." When the market continues down toward your breakeven point you think, "Hmm, this is not good, but at least I have not lost anything." Then it keeps on going down; you kick yourself and sell at a loss. Your $$$ is now $$.

Now what do you do? You have $$ of cash and need to find a new investment, so you start over and repeat the very same process again. You diligently do research and invest, and for a while the investment is working fine and the price goes up. You smile. But then the market stops going up, but you think, "I'm OK, I have a profit." When the market turns down toward your breakeven point you think, "Hmm, this

AVERAGE INVESTOR'S CURVE

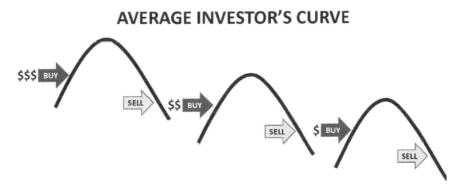

Figure 7 - By failing to anticipate the cyclical nature of markets, the average investor waits too long to sell, and a good investment turns bad.

is not good, but at least I have not lost anything." But when it keeps on going down, you kick yourself and sell at a loss. Your $$ is now $.

What do you do next? You now have $ of cash and have to find a new investment. Get the picture? This is what is presented in the Average Investor's Curve. This happens because the average investor does not have the insights or temperament to know when to buy and when to sell investments.

Temperament is much more important than intellect when it comes to being a successful investor. I know many Mensa members who are poor. Regardless of whether you have lots of brains or no brains, not aligning your investments with your temperament is a big problem.

LEARN FROM SUCCESSFUL INVESTORS, NOT YOUR MISTAKES

The most successful investors, legends like Peter Lynch, Sir John Templeton and Warren Buffett are really traders. They don't buy investments and just hope they do OK. They systematically cut losers from their portfolios. Some bought and sold their investments more often than others, but none were buy-and-hope-it-works-out investors. While managing the Fidelity Magellan fund in the 1970-80s, Peter Lynch's average holding period for his stocks was less than one year. Templeton normally had complete turnover in his portfolios about every 3-5 years.

Warren Buffett is fond of saying his favorite holding time is forever, but when an investment is not working out, he's not afraid to forget his own rule and sell, sell, sell. In 2017, he was selling Walmart (WMT), Suncor Energy (SU), Deer (DE), Charter Communications (CHTR) and Verisign (VRSN). Buffet is only a buy-and-hold investor for investments that keep performing. For all other investments, he is a hard-nosed trader. You can learn a lot from Warren Buffett!

Buffett has lost billions making mistakes like buying US Airways in 1989 and selling for 50 cents on the dollar. He lost $3 billion buying Conoco-Phillips in 2008 at the peak of the oil markets, lost $1.7 billion after Energy Future Holdings went bankrupt in 2013, and dropped $3.5 billion on Dexter Shoe Company, a 1993 purchase. Buffett's secret? He doesn't let the occasional loss stop him from selling and looking for a better opportunity. He keeps on going. That is the temperament of a winning investor.

However, over-trading can be just as big an impediment to investment success as not having the discipline to sell when an investment stops working. Day traders are notorious for losing money, but are hooked on the action, somewhat like compulsive gamblers. Like an addict or a workaholic, they can't conceive of not playing the markets with their systems. Some change systems as often as they change investments. They don't have the temperament to let winners stay in their portfolio to compound their returns year after year. They might be some of the brightest people around, but they have a compulsion to be overly active in trading and that is often the Achille's heel of those traders.

Good investment planning advice would include that you should only take risks that you need to take, and always be ready for change. If you have the temperament to plan for what to do when the investment environment changes, can recognize that change for what it is when it happens, and pull the trigger on the sale, then you probably can be a good investor.

Many who have the intellect to know how to plan for and identify changes can trip over ego-involved decisions. Suppose you find and buy what seems to be a great investment at a great price before it is discovered by the big players on Wall Street. If it begins to lose money, it is easy to talk yourself into thinking that it is only a matter of time before Wall Street gets as smart as you, so you wait instead of selling. If the price hits the "stop loss" sale triggering price you had set for the investment, it is tempting to think that this time it is different and walk away from your sell discipline.

Or perhaps you have an investment that hit the proverbial home run, maybe doubling in price. But it begins to decline. Do you blindly say, "Oh, it will come back" because it is your darling? Or, do you say, "It is down X% and that is my sell point," and pull the trigger on the sale? Personally, I always remind myself that if an investment does bounce back I can always buy back into it and have done so many times, but many investors don't react that way to their detriment.

Sometimes it is hard to see the forest through the trees, but investors must keep that clear vision that mounting losses are bad and should never be tolerated.

CUT YOUR MOUNTING LOSSES

In 2008, I made the mistake of launching my dream project, my own mutual fund. I discovered a terrific niche that no one else had been working, and designed a fund that was aimed at children's savings plans, Education IRAs, UTMA accounts, 529 College Savings Plans, etc. It was named the Kids Fund and focused on stocks of interest to children. Obvious names were Disney, Apple, Hasbro, Kellogg, and companies that kids might not recognize, like Unilever, which owns Popsicle, Ben and Jerry's, and Klondike Bars.

I planned and organized in 2007, and in 2008, I launched the fund. In hindsight I could not have picked a worse time. The financial crisis deepened, scaring everyone out of stocks. No one wanted to invest in anything new. Most people were selling, not buying. The brokerage community, which I had relied on to market the fund to investors with kids through their army of financial advisers, was so busy fending off lawsuits due to the fortunes they helped folks lose that looking at new investment offerings was very low on their priority list.

Mutual funds are very expensive to run, and involve a large number of lawyers, specialized accountants, daily pricing services, custodians, plus five-figure charges to be listed on mutual fund platforms such as Fidelity, Schwab, etc. By 2009, I was bleeding cash and despite putting up good performance numbers for the investments, I simply could not attract investors for the fund. I was rationalizing how great an idea it was and how much money I had tied up in the project that I really did not want to walk away from. I was convinced that soon the world would recognize my brilliant idea for what it was, and investor money would come flooding in for me to manage.

In one of those ah-ha moments, I realized that if a client had come to me with an investment that was not working, but was a terrific idea, sure to take off at some moment, with a large investment already having been made and they asked me for advice, I would have told them to cut their losses and move on. I often have frank conversations with clients in this situation that go like this, "Your investment money is spent and is no longer worth the original amount. Right now, you have $xxx. What is the best place for that money now? The current investment that is deteriorating or something else that is going up?"

At that moment, I realized that I had to take my own advice and close the fund. I felt like I had to put my faithful old dog to sleep. The decision was agonizing, but as soon as it was done I felt a relief and a freedom that I had not had in a couple of years.

This is a temperament marker. Can you get beyond the emotions of a losing trade or even a great winner and make the prudent decision? If so, you can be a successful investor. If not, consider hiring an investment manager who has this skill set, and importantly, the right temperament.

CHAPTER 9 – LOSE THE BUY-AND-HOPE-IT-WORKS-OUT MINDSET

"...the huge dollars involved in Wall Street support the most polished PR machine the world has ever known that spits out relentless waves of propaganda all reinforcing what they want you to do - be passive with your investments so they can bet against you when they please."

Will Hepburn

Buy-and-hold investing is by far the most used style of investing. Dozens of studies, articles and white papers have outlined the reasons for this, including:

- Statistical proof that buy-and-hold is a good long-term bet, often using 90-120 years of data.

- Calculations showing that buy-and-hold yields a higher overall return over long periods.

- Folksy aphorisms such as "the market goes up more often than it goes down."

Wall Street's favorite rationale for passive investing is the **Efficient Market Hypothesis** (EMH), a theory that states it is impossible to beat the market so don't even bother to try. Wall Street firms often seem to be saying, "Just leave your money with us. Be happy with average returns (if you are lucky) and leave us alone because we are big, and we are busy."

I would note that EMH was developed in the 1960s, and still remains just a theory. No one can prove the theory correct, but it has been repeated so often that it has taken on the aura of truth.

Wall Street can be so arrogant! They tell you that you might take big losses, but you can't do any better, so suck it up. How do they get away with it year after year? Because the huge dollars involved in Wall Street support the most polished PR machine the world has ever known that spits out relentless waves of propaganda all reinforcing what they want you to do - be passive about your investments so they can bet against you when they please.

The reinforcement of the passive, buy-and-hold message is repeated all up and down the food chain of the investment industry. Part of the reason for this begins with the individual investor - you. Passive, buy-and-hold is simple and easy for investors to understand. In an industry where things are so incredibly complicated and often seem backward if they can be deciphered at all, a simple, easy to understand approach is a powerful attraction.

And, buy-and-hold works often enough that Wall Street has numbers to point to and say "See! It works." The problem is that it does not work all the time and most investors and investment managers are not prepared for those times when it fails.

Wall Street firms know that investors lean toward softer and easier. Having clients hold investments for long periods makes Wall Street's life easier and more profitable, so their huge propaganda machine beats the drum of "buy-and-hold is the only way to go." If you are an investor searching for answers, you will encounter this message many times.

Most financial planners or investment advisers have business models built on promoting a passive, buy-and-hold approach because it is the easiest, lowest cost way for them to do business. They follow the path of least resistance and have incentives to not challenge the passive-is-better mindset of Wall Street. For new planners and advisers, promoting passive investments may be the only business model that they can put into action, so that is the way they go.

To change the foundation of one's business from buy-and-hold to an active focus is a lot like starting over. It is not easy to move into the business of being a proactive investment adviser. New skill sets must be gained. New technology is a must. Extra administrative support is needed. Considerable time is required, and clients often flee because they are used to being passive and are less comfortable with the idea of change. As a result, most advisers have strong incentives to maintain the status quo and keep promoting passive investing.

Industry regulators like the Financial Industry Regulatory Authority (FINRA), developed their mindset about trading years ago, during an era of high, fixed commission rates, when frequent trades could generate unsustainable costs that only benefited the broker. In that environment, it made sense to assume that investors should hold their commissioned investments for a long time to spread costs over longer time periods. While high, fixed commissions have disappeared, the mindset remains.

So, the primary regulator of the brokerage industry, FINRA, encourages buy-and-hold investing. The brokerage houses like buy-and-hold. Financial planners, brokers and advisers find buy-and-hold business models very easy to implement. Clients are comfortable with buy-and-hold because it is easy to understand. Buy-and-hold even performs well according to long-term studies, so why doesn't it work better?

WHAT COULD BE WRONG WITH THIS PICTURE?

The problem is that buy-and-hold only works well about half of the time. The rest of the time, it can become a disaster due to the relentless cycles of the market. Bear markets are a fact of investing. Wall Street would have investors merely whistle past the graveyard every time the bear is on the prowl.

An April 1, 2013, CNBC interview with John C. "Jack" Bogle is typical of Wall Street's callous attitude toward investors facing huge losses. Bogle is the founder and chairman of mutual-fund giant Vanguard Group and is widely credited for popularizing index funds, a staple for buy-and-hold investors.

CNBC anchor Scott Wapner put the question to Bogle: "You say, 'prepare for at least two declines of 25-30%, maybe even 50%, in the coming decade.' For a buy-and-hold guy, that's a little concerning, don't you think?"

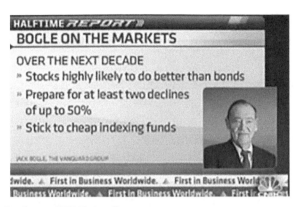

Figure 8 - Jack Bogle on CNBC, April 2013.

Bogle replied: "Not at all. They [bear markets] come and go. The market goes up, and the market goes down. It's never failed to recover from one of those 50% declines. I went through one in 1973-1974, I went through one in 2001, 2002, 2003; I went through another one 2008-2009. They're kind of scary – often terrifying – but it's typical."

Bogle's comments don't represent any shift in his philosophy – he remains as big a proponent of buy-and-hold investing as ever. Of course, his mutual funds have an infinite life, unlike you and I. Having your retirement fund cut in half by a stock market decline is a much bigger problem for you than for the mutual fund company.

If Bogle is right about two 50% declines in the next decade, it's going to be a tough time for those following his buy-and-hold advice. Wise investors will prepare for this kind of change and take action to move money out of harm's way when it begins.

Bear markets, defined by 20% or greater declines in the market, have occurred 33 times since 1900 according to Ned Davis Research. That is one bear market decline every 3.5 years. The average bear market lasts for 15 months, with stocks declining an average of 32% per Azzad Asset Management.

Remember, however, that averages can be deceiving. If I asked you if you would like to live in a place with an average year-round temperature of 70 degrees, how would that sound? It might sound like paradise until I tell you that average included three straight months of 90+ degree days with muggy conditions. This example is about the weather in New Orleans, and although I love New Orleans, summer weather there is surely not the reason. The average makes it sound pretty good though.

The reason I bring up averages is although the average bear market decline is 32%, according to the math of gains and losses this requires a 47% market rise to break even. The bear market of 2007-09 lasted 17 months and shaved a whopping 56% off the S&P 500 Index, requiring a 127% gain to recover.

How often do you see investments making a quick 47% gain? Occasionally? How often do you see investments make 127% gains? The answer is rarely and not quickly at all. Averages can be deceiving. As Mark Twain once said, "There are three kinds of lies: lies, damned lies, and statistics."

The long-term studies that the industry likes to tout are accurate in their statistics. Buy-and-hold investing might be fine for unfeeling pension funds or hedge funds with infinite life, but most individual investors find it too frustrating to spend three quarters of their time losing money and struggling to get back to break-even. They might need their money before the 90 or 120 years cited in many studies pass.

Let's use your personal retirement plan as an example. How long is your investment horizon? How long before you might want your money to fund retirement? 10 years? 20 years? Right now? You don't have 90 years or longer to let statistical averages assert themselves. So, let's look at what the reality is for us investors down here on Main Street.

Since the beginning of the year 2000 through 2017, the S&P 500 Index earned an average annual return of 3.39% (5.37% including dividends), less than half of what Wall Street's long-term studies would have you expect (Source: FastTrack). How would a huge shortfall in returns affect your retirement? Many pension funds in the U.S. are going broke because Wall Street said to expect 10% returns and delivered half of that at best.

In the past two decades, equity investors have had to endure two bear market declines that produced greater than 50% losses each time. If you had planned to retire in 2000, just before the first of these two bears began, it would have taken you 13 years to recover your retirement savings. 13 years of zero net return. Would that delay your retirement? It would for most folks.

If you had the misfortune of retiring just before one of these bear markets and were taking income from your investments while in a major decline, you had really big problems. Let's look at an example:

Assume you are 55 years old, have $1 million saved up and want to retire. $1 million is a nice nest egg, right? On, December 31, 1999, you retire expecting to withdraw $4,000 per month, or $48,000 annual income from your investments (4.8%), adjusted each year to keep up with 3% inflation. That is a basic withdrawal strategy recommended by Wall Street and many people go into retirement using it. Except, combining the subsequent bear market losses and withdrawals for living expenses, you would have run out of money in 2017 at age 72!

This is the kind of advice that Wall Street routinely dispenses and would have you follow. Does it sound like good advice? It doesn't to me.

MANAGING RISK IS CRITICAL TO SUCCESSFUL INVESTING

Stock markets involve inevitable cycles. Burying one's head in the sand and ignoring this fact, assuming that there will never be another bear market is a recipe for disappointment or disaster. If you invest this way and there is a bear market, even if you have the guts and deep pockets to ride it out, it leads to totally unnecessary losses.

Buy-and-hold proponents are not blind to the risk of market cycles and the pain of bear markets. But their tool to manage or limit this risk is severely flawed. To reduce risk in a passive portfolio one simply diversifies by investing in different asset classes that historically have moved in different directions in accordance with Modern Portfolio Theory, developed by Harry Markowitz in his paper, "Portfolio Selection," first published in 1952 by the *Journal of Finance*.

MPT states that for any level of risk one wishes to assume that there is a combination of investments that would have delivered the greatest return. By today's standards, MPT is a simple concept, but remember, it was developed back in the 1950s when most people had never seen a computer. They were considered wonder machines, sort of like the

Wizard of OZ pulling levers behind his curtain. Markowitz's computers were among the first to analyze many years of financial data on various investment categories combining them to manage risk. This was something that a human could not do back then and was considered ground-breaking work, so Markowitz was granted something akin to oracle status for his work.

For a time, MPT appeared to work as promised. It was unveiled during a period of generally rising markets. Diversifying the portfolio across a combination of investments from bonds to equities worked very well until the big bear markets in the 1970s, at which time its adherents took massive losses when many categories of investments all went down at the same time. The degree to which investments move in the same direction generally increases during market declines, rendering studies like MPT useless just when you need protection for your savings the most.

Because the markets have frequent cycles, I prefer to modify MPT to get more consistent returns by reducing investment in the categories MPT might suggest during bear markets and increasing them during bull markets. This is a simple, effective approach considered blasphemous by Wall Street and MPT adherents because the propaganda machine from Wall Street says you and I are not smart enough to know when to buy and sell. But we know better! Adjusting a portfolio to stay in sync with the realities of what the markets are doing at the moment can be a lifesaver during lousy markets.

I take MPT's basic premise which is diversification, and make it more effective by adjusting the allocations to the investment categories MPT identifies to be used. I do this by taking a MPT-type allocation and adapting that allocation to current market conditions.

As an example, if MPT said I would do well with 60% of my money in growth stocks, I would back that up with a system that would tell me when the market for growth stocks was strong or weak, so I could adjust my allocation from zero to 60%. I like allocations that can go from zero to 60 quickly when needed. It gives me a feeling like driving a powerful car. I can be out of growth stocks sitting in cash during bear markets, but fully invested during bull markets.

Investing can be a lot like driving your car. A buy-and-hold investor will put his money to work and then blindly stay in the same lane at the same speed. Even if he sees an accident ahead he will drive right into it. My enhanced Modern Portfolio Theory is like using the brakes and a steering wheel on your car when you see trouble ahead instead of piling into every accident that comes along in front of you. Having an investment adviser who manages your money proactively can be like riding in a limo where the driver can use the brakes and steering wheel to avoid trouble for your portfolio. It just makes sense to invest this way.

I have found that by enhancing Modern Portfolio Theory, my system can deliver much more consistent returns than an ordinary approach to MPT, and I encourage investors and investment advisers to consider adapting their portfolios to changing markets.

EXPLORE ALTERNATIVES TO MODERN PORTFOLIO THEORY

If bear markets involve sharp declines and rapid recoveries, doesn't it make sense to step aside when bear markets, such as Vanguard founder Jack Bogle anticipates, become evident? Then, step back into the market when the recovery is underway? Certainly, it does. However, that sounds a lot like the market timing that Wall Street and the media vilify, doesn't it?

The media, doing Wall Street's bidding, mischaracterizes proactive trading as market timing in which one must pick exact market tops or bottoms to be successful. That is far from the truth of what most proactive money managers really do. Proactive investors follow general probabilities that are rarely black and white. The stock market goes up around 51% of the days it is open. So, all we need to go from an average investor to a successful one are systems to keep us invested for the majority of the rising days and out of the market the majority of days when prices fall.

In the following chapters, I will show you several simple systems that anyone can implement to help you escape the grip of the Wall Street propaganda machine and be invested during strong markets and in a safe harbor during weak markets. It's simple, really.

CHAPTER 10 – THE EDGE PROVIDED BY PROACTIVE INVESTING

"The easiest way to make money is to have more money in asset classes that are going up, and less in asset classes that are going down."

Will Hepburn

Whether we realize it or not, studies show that mass marketing has a tremendous impact on us, especially if we are investors. It seems every week, I hear a market expert touting the benefits of long-term passive investing. While returns from passive investing have clearly proven to be anything but reliable, Wall Street's propaganda machine continues the drum beat of "buy-and-hold is the only good way to invest."

Investors are usually shocked to learn that most industry professionals and their firms actively manage their own portfolios while they continue to discourage their individual clients from doing the same. I see it as a lack of commitment on their part. A passive buy-and-hold strategy is cheap and easy to deliver. Providing clients with advice that requires action in response to market conditions is more expensive and time consuming, and requires a higher degree of skill. Most investment firms are simply not willing to put forth the necessary effort to provide for their clients' investments like they do their own. Instead, they recommend what is easy, the road most traveled; the same one down which the vast majority of investment firms send their investors – I call it the road of buy-and-hope.

While investment firms claim to be independent, the investment philosophy they sell is often similar. The benefit, of course, is that when things go wrong there's comfort and job security in being part of the crowd. How many financial advisers have been fired for holding stock in GE, Microsoft, or Pfizer, despite taking huge losses at times? Not many. Misery loves company.

Another reason mainstream investment firms tout buy-and-hold has to do with their ability to sell the concept. A simple concept like buy-and-hold-forever is easy to sell compared to the more complex active management approach focusing on risk management. The faster they can sell one client, the faster they can get to the next one. These firms are in business to make a profit, and their time is money.

INVESTING ONLY WITH AN OFFENSE

Being part of the buy-and-hold crowd is like playing a football game with only half your team on the field. What if you were the owner of a football team that was limited to fielding only an offense – no defense! How likely is it that your team will be successful over the course of the season? Investing is like football in that the winners normally play good defense as well as good offense.

Unfortunately, a one-dimensional approach is what many investors use today. They have been convinced by promotions that an investment designed only to profit in bull markets will ultimately bring them success. They've been taught to ignore the fact that they have no way to profit or protect their assets during declining markets.

Looking at the last 50 years, you might be surprised to learn that on a daily basis the stock market finished down 48% of the time! This is one reason that prudent investing requires a defensive plan as well as an offensive plan.

WHEN TO USE A PASSIVE APPROACH

In what areas of your life do you normally pursue clear goals using a passive approach rather than a proactive one?

- ◆ How about in raising your children? Is it a good idea to be passive? Not really.
- ◆ What about in advancing your career? Would it be a good idea to be passive while attempting to climb the corporate ladder? Probably not.
- ◆ Well, how about on the athletic field? Would a passive approach work in your favor? Of course not. Rarely does an athlete with a passive attitude succeed.

Why then, do so many financial professionals promote the idea of passive investing? It amazes me.

PROACTIVE MANAGEMENT'S EDGE

The passive approach to investing is doomed to fail at some point. Passive buy-and-hold strategies work pretty well in rising markets – but they always fail during falling markets. Buy-and-hold investing is like any other form of gambling; eventually your luck runs out. As John Kenneth Galbraith, noted 20th century economist, told us: "The longer one holds a stock, the more certain it becomes that he will encounter a significant market upheaval. Risk does not go down with time, it goes up!"

Time brings greater price fluctuations. Passive strategies continually expose assets to these market fluctuations and disappoint investors when markets decline. Passive strategies attempt to ride out the declines, betting that markets will be higher not lower when the investor needs his or her money.

Having investments that can adapt to market conditions is clearly sensible and safer. Although there is no perfect investment strategy, no silver bullet, and no guru who always gets it right, strategies that *Adapt to Changing Markets*® all have one thing in common. They strive to provide investors with an edge on the market they would not enjoy with a passive buy-and-hold style.

This edge can be as simple as selling investments and moving to cash when declines reach a certain point; only buying investments that are going up in price, or following pricing patterns that have had some success as predictors of future activity. There are many different styles of proactive management, each pursuing a different advantage.

Diversification means not keeping all of your eggs in one basket. Having only one strategy for investing is much like only owning one stock. Lack of diversification increases one's risk.

Proactive management means making decisions. Your decisions won't always be correct, but that doesn't mean you shouldn't keep trying to do what is right. If you are uncomfortable making these decisions for yourself, consider hiring a proactive money manager to oversee your portfolio for you. You aren't passive about other areas in your life in which you hope to excel – investing should be no different.

If you think about it, doing nothing is a strategy, probably a cousin to buy-and-hope-it-works-out, but there are also many ways to invest proactively and each proactive strategy provides an edge that can increase your chance of investing success.

Proactive does not mean day trading, where you have to watch your portfolios every day. However, being proactive will require you to look at your accounts periodically to be sure the market conditions that favor your investment haven't changed. This period can be as long as quarterly if you choose a longer-term strategy. If you can't look after your investments at least quarterly, you may be better off hiring a professional money manager to do this for you. Chapter 19 will give you insights into the type of manager to look for and what to expect them to do for your portfolio.

Just as you will get better service from your lawyer if you understand and can discuss the issues, and from your mechanic if you can accurately describe what you want fixed, you will get better results from your investment adviser if you know how to tell them what you want and are able to know if those are the results you are getting – or not. Reading this book will help you with this, even if you decide to delegate your investment management to a professional.

CHAPTER 11 - DIVERSIFICATION AND PROACTIVE MANAGEMENT

"Diversification is a little like playing poker. Most of us know that three of a kind beats a pair, but to play well enough to consistently win money playing poker takes a whole different level of knowledge and skill. Investing works the same way."

Will Hepburn

Diversification is like owning more than one pair of shoes. When one pair gets wet, you can wear the dry pair. Like many simple concepts, diversification is often misunderstood and not implemented effectively.

In analyzing thousands of portfolios over the past 30-some years, one of the most common mistakes I see is two-dimensional diversification applied in three-dimensional markets. Let me explain.

Basic diversification is a pretty simple concept – spread your risk so that no single problem should be able to wipe out your entire portfolio.

The traditional financial planning approach would suggest not keeping all your money in one asset class, such as stocks or bonds. Owning both classes of investments provides the first dimension of safety for your money since the stock and bond markets are less likely to both turn down at the same time.

To add a second dimension of diversification, don't just own one bond or stock, own several, so if one goes bust, your entire nest egg is not wiped out.

Stopping after this two-dimensional approach to diversification can lead to unnecessary losses because you will be failing to recognize that investment markets change. Your portfolio needs to be ready to change, too. This requires a third level of diversification - by strategy.

Most investors, and sadly most financial advisers, aren't even aware of the many strategies beyond "buy-and-hope things work out." To illustrate this point, let's do a short quiz.

How many investment strategies can you name? Quick, now!

If you have trouble naming alternatives to buy-and-hold, your diversification may only be two-dimensional and your investments taking needless risk. The level of losses you incurred in the last big market decline can confirm this for you.

Don't feel alone. Wall Street discourages doing anything beyond simple buying of investments. They don't want you to ever sell. Most investors have never been taught that there is something called strategy diversification, so they have never thought about different strategies.

Certain strategies work best in different stages of a business cycle, and no single strategy works in all parts of a cycle. A strategy that works well in rising markets, such as buy-and-hold, rarely works well in a declining market. Buy-and-hold is a growth strategy, and a decent one at that. You might have noticed that I often make critical comments of buy-and-hold, but my criticism is only aimed at those who try to use buy-and-hold in all markets, because it does nothing to preserve capital in down markets. It only works about half the time – when the market is going up. The rest of the time, it may be a recipe for disaster.

Simplistic buy-and-hold lacks a sell strategy, and everyone needs to know when to sell. Consider the Enron investors who were wiped out in 2001. They did not have a bad investment. Enron had gone up over 1000%! I don't know about you, but I consider an investment that grows to ten times its original value to be a good one. What those investors who were ruined in Enron's collapse lacked was a strategy to tell them when to sell.

Make no mistake, doing nothing is a strategy, but it is not a good one.

If you believe, as I do, that the three most important rules in investing are *don't lose your money, don't lose your money, don't lose your money*, then at times you must pursue capital preservation or pay a big price.

In down markets, preserving your account values becomes the name of the game, so changing your strategy can save you a lot. Several times in my career I have been able to show my clients periods where I saved them 10 times my annual fee by being proactive with their accounts, by shifting from growth to capital preservation and back as called for by market conditions.

If you only have strategies that work well in bull markets, that can still work ok. Just be prepared to move to cash during market declines to preserve your capital. Sitting in cash or a money market fund during declines is just fine. In fact, holding cash is a superior strategy when the market is tanking. When the decline is over and the market begins to recover, you should be able to buy many more shares of the companies you held earlier, now at bargain-basement prices. What counts is not the tiny interest the money market fund pays during the stock market decline but the fact that your cash then buys many more shares for you.

This is called relative value, and it is a valuable tool when the prices of assets are fluctuating.

ASSET CLASS DIVERSIFICATION IS NOT A STRATEGY

Diversification is often mentioned as a strategy, and, true, it is a risk control mechanism that is often used in buy-and-hold portfolios to reduce risk. However, it is an add-on to a buy-and-hold portfolio and not really the proactive investment strategy that we are looking for here.

Wall Street would have you diversify your investments over several asset classes and then tell you to leave them alone. They might dust off an old study that says 92% of investment returns come from the choice of asset classes that you invest in, such as value stocks, tech stocks, energy stocks, bonds, etc. Stock selection and market timing only account for 8% of the returns, according to this theory, so don't even bother with those details, the fund companies would tell you. Just put your money in their hands and let them worry about the finer points for you. Like so much faulty advice from Wall Street, this is built upon a kernel of truth that the propaganda machine twists to their benefit.

My interpretation of this study (Brinson, Beebower and Hood, 1992 if you care to look it up) is that 92% of investment gains come from being in the right asset classes, but also 92% of losses come from being in the wrong ones. When the markets change, you need to change, too, or you will lose money, studies or no studies.

PROACTIVE STRATEGIES ADD DEFENSE TO YOUR PLAY BOOK

Proactive strategies will tell you when to sell as well as when to buy, when to take action, when to play defense. Defense wins the big football games, and it is the same in investing. Investors who can play a little defense usually do better.

We aren't going to go into all of them in this book, but investment strategies come in many categories such as

- Growth or Value,
- Sector Rotation,
- Contrarian,
- Arbitrage,
- Long-Short,
- Market Neutral,
- Trend Following,
- Seasonality,
- Wave Analysis,
- Market Timing,
- Pair Trading, and many others.

A trait all these strategies share is that they are systems that tell investors when it is time to adapt to changes in the markets. Not every signal will be successful. And there will be times when the strategies fail to protect your assets the way you might want. However, your alternative is waiting for the train wreck that has come at the end of every market cycle.

If more investors had used strategies that could adapt to changes in the markets when bear markets occur, life altering financial damage could have been averted in the big declines we have mentioned. Do you know anyone whose retirement has been negatively impacted by market losses? I'm guessing those people did not have a plan for what to do if an investment started to act differently than expected, and this is a major reason why bad things can happen to good investments.

Remember, the great American investment creed, "buy low, sell high," is a two-part goal. It is not "buy, period," as many Wall Street institutions would have you think.

Diversification is a little like playing poker. Most of us know that three of a kind beats a pair, but to play well enough to consistently win money playing poker takes a whole different level of knowledge and skill. Investing works the same way.

Effective use of various strategies requires a different level of knowledge and skill beyond buy-and-hold. You may need professional help, but it will be well worth the time and expense, especially the next time the markets hit the skids.

More market declines will be coming, that is for sure. The question is, will your portfolio be able to handle them the next time? There are many types of proactive management strategies that can tell you when to sell and what to buy. We will go through some of them in the next chapters.

CHAPTER 12 - NON-TECHNICAL APPROACHES TO PROACTIVE INVESTING

"Proactive management strategies can tell you how to adapt to changes in the market when your investments get off track, which from my perspective is a heck of a lot better than just wringing my hands and waiting for the market to recover."

Will Hepburn

I like to say that the easiest way to make money is to have more money in asset classes that are going up, and less in asset classes that are going down. One way to accomplish this is to look at your statements, at least quarterly, and see what is going up and what is going down. Combine that information with a sell strategy and the willingness to sell when your investments are losing value, and you are ahead of the average investor.

In future chapters, I look at more technical strategies for investing proactively, but before we get there, let's look at some non-technical approaches.

ADAPTIVE REBALANCING USING THE NAAIM EXPOSURE INDEX

One of the simplest strategies an investor can implement piggy backs on the collective skills of the professional managers who are members of NAAIM, the National Association of Active Investment Managers.

Few professional money managers want anyone peeking over their shoulder into their decision-making process because that is their intellectual property. They protect it fiercely. However, NAAIM managers report their current exposure to the stock market to their association headquarters as part of a project that began in 2006. Data are compiled each week into the latest NAAIM Number, which tells the members' current overall exposure to the stock market. This number is then used to create the NAAIM Exposure Index. This Index can give us some valuable insights.

NAAIM managers might be fully invested (100% in stocks), lightly invested (perhaps 40% in stocks), and even short the stock market - where they intend to make money if the stock market goes down (0% or less in stocks). You can see this in the weekly NAAIM Numbers. By comparing the current NAAIM Number to the previous week's data, we can see when these professional money managers, as a group, are getting more bullish or more bearish on the stock market.

Hundreds of newsletter writers, financial websites and market analysts follow this data, and it has become a respected market indicator. Analysts like Tom McClellan of the McClellan Market Report (http://www.mcoscillator.com) have noted that when the NAAIM Exposure Index is declining (becoming more conservative) and the stock market is rising, it is usually the Exposure Index that is right.

Let's take a look at what you can do to adjust your stock/bond allocation to stay in sync with what the market is actually doing by using the NAAIM Number. Instead of ordinary rebalancing to a traditional 60/40 mix of stocks and bonds, let's adjust your stock holdings once a quarter to match the previous quarter's average of the NAAIM Exposure Index allocating the rest to bonds. A study that my firm conducted in 2010 and updated in 2017, shows how you would have done by following this easy system.

The study used S&P 500 market returns beginning on 9/30/2006 - the first full quarter of the NAAIM Exposure Index, through 9/30/2017, during which the S&P 500 stock index went through several complete market cycles. It is important to always look at investments and strategies in both up and down cycles to judge how they work.

During this period, the Quarterly Average NAAIM Number ranged from a growth oriented 87% stock allocation on March 27, 2013 to a capital preservation allocation of 12% exposure to stocks on December

31, 2008. Considering that the stock market went down another 11% during the last months of the market crash, which would you rather be holding, a 60% stock portfolio stuck in a buy-and-hold strategy that had been horribly beaten up during the previous 12 months, or adapting to the market and holding only 12% in stocks? Personally, I'd much rather be out during a sharp market decline, wouldn't you?

In full disclosure, the NAAIM Number during the heart of the financial crisis, from 1/1/2008 until 3/31/2009, would have given us an average allocation of 38% in stocks, still a lot better on the wallet than holding the industry standard 60% in stocks. During the 4th quarter of 2008 and first quarter of 2009 when the bear market had really picked up steam, the NAAIM Number was 22% and 12% respectively. This simple system really dodged financial bullets in 2008-09.

As a result of avoiding the financial carnage the stock market was delivering in 2007-09, the returns during the full 11-year period of the study increased from 7.02% annual average return for 60% stocks/40% bonds mix to an 8.85% gain using the suggested form of adaptive rebalancing over the period of the study. That is a 20% greater return from the proactive strategy. Significantly, the NAAIM allocation was profitable in the 4th quarter of 2008 when the markets and the investments of many investors were taking huge losses due to the financial crisis in the U.S.

Looking at risk, the increase in returns is even more striking. The maximum loss from the NAAIM allocation was 13.62% during the study, while the 60/40 portfolio lost twice as much, dropping 27.18% of its value, even while holding 40% in bonds. These loss figures represent the drawdown in value from the highest point to the lowest point before recovering, and demonstrate the dramatically reduced risk of pursuing growth using the NAAIM allocation.

Because we only measured quarter-end returns, day-to-day volatility for both portfolios would probably have been greater than what is presented here, but if you only look at your statements quarterly, day-to-day volatility may not bother you much. Clearly, this simple, easy system delivered better results with less risk than buy-and-hold.[‡]

[‡] Past performance is no guarantee of future results.

If you want better returns with half the risk, now you know one way you may get it. All you may have to do is buy or sell a small amount of your stock funds each quarter to stay in sync with the NAAIM Exposure Index quarterly average. NAAIM even posts the quarterly average of the NAAIM Number for investor and adviser use. Check out the data at https://www.naaim.org/programs/naaim-exposure-index/

While we are at it, let's look at another simple strategy that you can do without needing a math degree or a Wall Street background.

A SIMPLE GUIDE TO BUYING AND SELLING EARNINGS

Another simple way to buy low and sell high is following the earnings of companies that you own by periodically looking at PE ratios, which is shorthand for Price to Earnings ratios. PE ratios show how much you have to pay for each dollar of earnings.

For instance, in September 2017, Exxon had a PE of 29, meaning you have to pay $29 for $1 of earnings. This is much higher than Exxon's historic average PE of around 10. For many years prior to 2013, you could have bought $1 of Exxon earnings for $10 or less. A PE of 10 sounds pretty cheap now, but we can't deal with an exercise in "if only." We deal with today's reality.

What changed? Either the price of Exxon has risen a lot (it hasn't) or its earnings per share have dropped a lot (which they have). To correct this imbalance, one of three things needs to happen:

(1)   Exxon's earnings need to rise dramatically, or
(2)   Its price drops dramatically, or
(3)   A combination of both.

In two out of those three situations you will lose money holding Exxon stock. If you find yourself in a situation like this, I would suggest that it is time to invest elsewhere, unless you just feel lucky.

This particular change in earnings for Exxon was caused by the huge oil supplies that were beginning to flow from the fracking industry, affecting the supply/demand balance in the oil markets. This pushed the price of oil down, taking Exxon's profits with it.

However, you did not have to be an industry analyst to figure this out. You could have seen it coming as early as the end of 2013 when PE ratios first broke above the 10 mark and never went back down.

To protect your investment, you did not have to be right on top of Exxon stock data nor did you have to react quickly to this change either, because Exxon's stock price stayed up for several quarters after the PE ratio moved higher. Merely checking the PE ratio vs. its historic level for Exxon stock would have shown you a red flag and told you that it was a good time to sell high. If you only get the "sell high" half of the great American investment creed correct, you can do very well.

PE ratios and a wealth of other data can be seen for free on StockCharts.com, Yahoo Finance, FINVIZ.com, Google Finance and more places. Every time you buy a stock make a note or save a screen shot of its pertinent data like PE ratios. This will give you a valuable reference point later when evaluating your investment.

Let's look at an example of how this works by assuming you want to buy shares in a large pharmaceutical company, but you don't know which one is the best deal. A free site like FINVIZ.com will have a screener, which will allow you to bring up a list of drug manufacturers in seconds. With one click on the PE column you can sort by PE ratio and see that as of December 31, 2017, PEs in this industry currently run from a low of 22 to a high of 66. At the time this screen was run, Johnson & Johnson had a PE of 24. If you are comfortable buying Johnson & Johnson, you now know that you are getting one of the least expensive of the major drug companies. You can sleep well knowing that at least you have done the "buy low" part of the investment creed well.

In my college classes, I discuss index fund investing and point out that few investors would want to own an index fund if given a close look at many of the stocks in the index. The real stinkers (technical term, there) might be on their way out of business altogether, and the high flyers might have outrageously high PE ratios, if they have earnings at all. They are in the index because they are needed to enable the index to represent all stocks in the category. You would probably never want to buy them if you looked at these stinkers individually. PE ratios are among the easiest ways to weed funky stocks out.

This simple system for buying low and selling high can be applied to index mutual funds or ETFs, too. Let's look through our PE lens at the nine individual sectors of the S&P 500 to see if we can get a hint of what we should be selling or buying.

At the end of 2017, the S&P 500 Index had an overall PE of 22.88. The nine sectors shown below comprise all 500 of the S&P stocks, so you might expect many of the sectors to sport PE ratios close to the index average, and most do. However, Energy takes $36.10 to buy $1 of earnings, so it looks pretty expensive compared to Financials, where you can buy $1 of earnings for only $17.30.

Table 8 - PE ratios for the nine sectors of the S&P 500 Index, December 2017.

Nine Sectors of the S&P 500 Index

Symbol	Name	PE Ratio
XLF	Financial Select Sector SPDR Fund	17.3
XLV	Health Care Select Sector SPDR Fund	17.7
XLU	Utilities Select Sector SPDR Fund	18.2
XLK	Technology Select Sector SPDR Fund	20.7
XLI	Industrial Select Sector SPDR Fund	21.6
XLP	Consumer Staples Select Sector SPDR Fund	21.6
XLB	Materials Select Sector SPDR ETF	21.7
XLY	Consumer Discretionary Select Sector SPDR Fund	23.1
XLE	Energy Select Sector SPDR Fund	36.1

If you are a value investor, you now have a good idea of what sectors to avoid, and what sectors to put your extra money into. This simple system takes very little tending - quarterly is fine - and it often provides better returns than buying and holding an S&P 500 Index Fund.

Many value investors focus on earnings; using the PE ratio as a guide is a very simple way to do this.

So now you have two proactively managed strategies that will take very little of your time, and each has the potential to outperform passive buy-and-hold investing, while reducing risk at the same time.

SEASONALITY STRATEGIES – SELL IN MAY AND GO AWAY

It seems that Rev. Jesse Jackson believes anything that he can make rhyme just has to be true, a trait sometimes referred to as the Jacksonian Fallacy. Humans do tend to believe more in statements that rhyme, perhaps because they are a bit more memorable. So, Rev. Jackson may be onto something even if it is not the truth. Johnny Cochran made this tactic famous with his *"If it doesn't fit, you must acquit"* line, referring to the glove in OJ Simpson's trial.

The old stock market adage *"Sell in May and Go Away"* refers to the idea that there is not much money to be made in stocks after May 1st so one might as well do nothing. It does work in many years, but probably not just because it rhymes. The seasonal market peak actually occurs as late as August 1st, but it is hard to find a word that rhymes with "August."

Many people believed that this seasonality is caused by the lower volume of activity on Wall Street as many rich traders go on summer vacations. But as with most things on Wall Street, it is due to money flows. Trading volume does not drop much in summer, but observable money flows do drop off in summer. So, let's follow the money, as the old saying goes, to see what drives this seasonal tendency.

In the fall, factories begin gearing up for Christmas. More workers get hired, more truck drivers are needed to deliver things and more clerks are needed to sell the goods. All this economic activity gets money moving in the economy and some of that money starts finding its way into the financial markets through 401k plans and other savings.

Around the end of the year come mutual fund distributions. Profit sharing payments and tax refunds occur during the first month or two of the new year, events that put money into consumer's hands, some of which also finds its way into the financial markets.

In the spring, the money flows into the stock markets ebb and begin to flow the other way. Folks who did not get tax refunds earlier now get to write big checks to the government.

The largest influence on this money flow, however, is home sales. Were you aware that more people buy homes in the summer than winter? They do. So, where do you think that house money was before it is put down on a house? It comes from stocks, bonds, mutual funds, and savings. This money flows out of the financial markets into real estate during summer.

The simple explanation for this warm weather/cold weather bias in the markets is that during warmer months there is just less money that people can devote to the stock market.

How persistent is this phenomenon? On the next page are the results looking back to 1984. I took the S&P 500 closing prices and lumped them into warmer, May 1st - Oct 31st, blocks and colder, November 1st to April 30th, blocks. The stronger of the six-month periods for the year is highlighted.

Since 1984, for the S&P 500, 20 out of 33 cooler six-month periods have outperformed the six warmer months that preceded them. That is a 60% accuracy rating. Ignoring the years in which distortion was caused by the real estate bubble leading to the 2007-08 financial crisis, this ratio becomes 20 out of 28 years that colder periods outperformed warmer ones, or a 71% accuracy for this indicator. Examining the 30 stocks of the Dow Jones Industrial Average's seasonality over this same period, colder periods have outperformed warmer periods 70% of the time.

Considering that the stock market goes up slightly more than half of the time, a simple strategy that can produce 60 or 70% wins can improve your performance significantly.

More importantly, when the colder months outperform, they do so by a much wider margin than warmer months. Simply adding the six-month returns from 1984, the warmer months produced a gain of 63.34% and the colder months produced a gain of 253.42%, four times the gain in warmer months.

Table 9 - Seasonality returns for warm versus cold months of the year.

S&P 500 Returns for:

6 Months Ending			6 Months Ending		
10/31/1984	8.65%	Warmer	4/30/1985	15.88%	Colder
10/31/1985	6.66%	Warmer	4/30/1986	22.35%	Colder
10/31/1986	0.76%	Warmer	4/30/1987	16.40%	Colder
10/31/1987	-20.61%	Warmer	4/30/1988	13.83%	Colder
10/31/1988	4.40%	Warmer	4/30/1989	17.11%	Colder
10/31/1989	7.95%	Warmer	4/30/1990	4.40%	Colder
10/31/1990	-10.80%	Warmer	4/30/1991	20.98%	Colder
10/31/1991	-3.75%	Warmer	4/30/1992	10.70%	Colder
10/31/1992	3.85%	Warmer	4/30/1993	4.37%	Colder
10/31/1993	2.58%	Warmer	4/30/1994	-1.15%	Colder
10/31/1994	-0.62%	Warmer	4/30/1995	17.57%	Colder
10/31/1995	13.49%	Warmer	4/30/1996	10.53%	Colder
10/31/1996	13.14%	Warmer	4/30/1997	12.06%	Colder
10/31/1997	12.63%	Warmer	4/30/1998	14.17%	Colder
10/31/1998	6.67%	Warmer	4/30/1999	11.88%	Colder
10/31/1999	6.69%	Warmer	4/30/2000	2.28%	Colder
10/31/2000	-7.44%	Warmer	4/30/2001	-4.50%	Colder
10/31/2001	-9.27%	Warmer	4/30/2002	-6.35%	Colder
10/31/2002	-12.26%	Warmer	4/30/2003	2.91%	Colder
10/31/2003	9.82%	Warmer	4/30/2004	5.90%	Colder
10/31/2004	4.74%	Warmer	4/30/2005	1.51%	Colder
10/31/2005	4.87%	Warmer	4/30/2006	1.65%	Colder
10/31/2006	10.28%	Warmer	4/30/2007	9.28%	Colder
10/31/2007	-3.23%	Warmer	4/30/2008	-5.45%	Colder
10/31/2008	-36.0%	Warmer	4/30/2009	2.56%	Colder
10/31/2009	19.20%	Warmer	4/30/2010	-0.57%	Colder
10/31/2010	8.37%	Warmer	4/30/2011	13.95%	Colder
10/31/2011	-7.30%	Warmer	4/30/2012	5.08%	Colder
10/31/2012	8.08%	Warmer	4/30/2013	15.15%	Colder
10/31/2013	10.74%	Warmer	4/30/2014	6.52%	Colder
10/31/2014	7.49%	Warmer	4/30/2015	1.93%	Colder
10/31/2015	-1.28%	Warmer	4/30/2016	0.80%	Colder
10/31/2016	4.86%	Warmer	4/30/2017	9.69%	Colder
	63.34%	Gains		**253.42%**	Gains

One of the many reasons for this big imbalance in returns is that money flows had been tapering off for many months prior to the historic stock market crashes, which occurred at the end of the warmer six-month periods. If we look back to the biggest stock market declines in history, 1929, 1987, 2001 or 2008, each of these happened in September or October. It should be no surprise that economic shocks are felt much harder in markets that are already weakened by poor money flows.

This tells us that the warmer months not only produce fewer winning periods but also include most of the really ugly stock markets. If you think about this, why would anyone want to stay fully invested all summer long? It just does not make sense, unless one has never seen the actual data. Funny how Wall Street never mentions this except to repeat their little ditty each May 1st.

Let's apply the math of gains and losses to a $100,000 investment in the Dow from November 1953 through the end of April 2017. Here is how returns would look to a buy-and-hold investor, compared to the results someone would achieve by investing only in the colder months or only in the warmer months, with their portfolios in cash the remainder of the year:

Date	Buy-and-hold	Colder Months	Warmer Months
Nov. 1, 1953	$ 100,000	$ 100,000	$ 100,000
May 1, 2017	$ 7,197,208	$ 6,590,965	$ 109,198

Some segments of the markets are not affected by this seasonality nor are some regions, so blindly following the May 1 to November 1 time frames presented in this simple example is probably not a good idea. The late analyst Sy Harding did several studies showing that the earliest the seasonal influence gets traction in the spring is April 21st, and the earliest it ended was October 16th. Harding used technical indicators that told him when the change actually occurred. Tom McClellan, editor of the *McClellan Market Report*, has done studies that show that the average seasonal peak price in warmer months occurs on August 1st.

There is a simple way to take advantage of this clear seasonal tendency, and that is to either have a proactive strategy in place to detect when money flows are changing and move money out of harm's way in warmer months or hire someone who does. I have found that one simple tactic is to be aware of these seasonal tendencies and be ready to sell weaker investments as they lose strength during the summer and wait to reinvest that money until after the weather cools down.

As we learn from the old story about the man who drowned crossing a lake that averaged only three-feet deep, averages can be deceiving. Taking action on the average dates mentioned above won't always work.

THE PRESIDENTIAL CYCLE

In addition to the seasonal cycle, there is also a four-year cycle based upon the presidential elections. We begin counting presidential years on election day in early November through the next November, so it takes some mental gymnastics to track them for the effect on your portfolio.

The first year of a presidential cycle - especially for newly elected presidents who enact many programs that can create uncertainty - usually produces a weak year in stock market terms. Investors hate uncertainty and when it is present will begin to hold back, tilting the balance of buyers and sellers slightly. The second year in the cycle has a reputation for producing sharp stock market declines as a stream of negative news over new presidential programs deepens the uncertainty.

The third year in a presidential cycle is when things begin to brighten. Gains from the low in the second year of a president's term to the high in year three are the strongest of the four-year period. The fourth years are often good as the polish the administration puts on everything in order to get re-elected is in full effect.

Knowing these annual tendencies can give you an edge over the average investor by suggesting you invest for growth in presidential years 3-4 and more conservatively in years 1-2.

The late Marty Zweig said, *"Never fight the [ticker] tape,"* meaning the trend of the market. The market has some fairly clear seasonal trends that investors can follow to their advantage, but they have to realize that to be a successful investor means one must know when to move their money to safety and be willing to do that.

So now you have four proactively managed strategies that will take very little of your time, each with the potential to outperform passive buy-and-hold investing, while reducing risk at the same time.

Keep in mind that these proactive management strategies are not perfect, merely good. They can tell you how to adapt to changes in the market when your investments get off track, which from my perspective is a heck of a lot better than just wringing my hands waiting for the market to recover. Even if you are on the right track, if you just sit there long enough you will get run over by a train.

The science of proactive management involves understanding the various strategies available. There are many more ways to manage money than the strategies presented here. The art of managing money is knowing when to apply various strategies. Just as having a scalpel does not make you a surgeon, just knowing about a few different strategies does not make you a money manager.

If this type of investing intrigues you, but you don't really understand it or may not have the discipline to monitor your investments as your strategy requires, consider hiring a professional money manager to do it for you.

CHAPTER 13 - INVESTOR SENTIMENT AND THE FINANCIAL MARKET

"...don't watch the hand the magician wants you to see. Watch what else is happening."

Will Hepburn

As a child I was a good swimmer and vividly remember the cliff divers in Acapulco, who had to time their dives from high on a cliff into a narrow inlet with each wave. If they jumped when the water covered the rocks, the wave would recede before they landed, and they would be smashed on the rocks below. They had to jump while the rocks were showing, having faith that a few seconds later a wave would be there to cover the rocks. Talk about courage!

The financial markets are merely an ebb and flow of the balance between buyers and sellers, similar to the ebb and flow of water over the rocks below the cliff divers of Acapulco. The flow is often counter intuitive, somewhat like *jump when you see rocks,* but really it is more like *don't watch the hand the magician wants you to see, watch what else is happening.*

It may seem odd to look at financial markets as sentimental, but investor sentiment is a useful gauge of the possible future direction of a market. True, no one knows exactly what the market will do on any particular day. Short-term events are often driven by the daily news and frequently make no sense at all.

However, longer term, the financial markets are driven by supply and demand – the relationship in the numbers of buyers and sellers at any one point in time. When this relationship is in balance, prices will be stable. When buyers outnumber sellers, prices rise. When sellers outnumber buyers, prices decline. Price declines can be caused either when buyers become uncertain and hold back, or sellers show up in larger numbers than normal. When both happen at the same time, prices can drop quickly. Economics 101.

CONTRARY NATURE OF SENTIMENT INDICATORS

Sentiment indexes report the feelings of different groups of market players such as investors, money managers or newsletter writers. When sentiment comes into play, it can often seem backward, like so many things in this business do. More important than the actual sentiment numbers that are reported is the potential for change represented by the numbers.

Bullish people invest their money because they believe the market is strong. Reports that the numbers of bullish investors or managers has risen sound encouraging on the surface, but let's analyze what is really happening. The number of investors who like the market is high. Normally those same investors, if they like the market, will have put their money where their mouth is and are invested. So far this makes sense.

However, bullish sentiment numbers are often telling us that it is actually time to sell, not buy as you might think, because the number of people who have already invested their money has risen. When you think about this, you will realize that those who have invested their money are no longer potential buyers but have now become potential sellers. When the number of potential sellers is greater than the number of potential buyers, a condition is created from which markets move lower. At this point, all that is needed for the market to decline is some of that daily news that can drive prices down for no apparent reason.

It works the other way when everyone is bearish on the market. This indicates a shortage of potential sellers because everyone has already sold. There is lots of cash on the sidelines, which often acts like rocket fuel for stock prices when a market turns around and buyers invest their cash.

Sentiment indicators are sometimes categorized wrongly as "contrary indicators" implying that the people polled are ignorant and always wrong, which is far from the truth. Those who use that label just can't see beyond the surface of the numbers and understand what they mean – or they don't want you to understand it. This may be another face of the Wall Street propaganda machine trying to get you to take the unprofitable side of an investment so they can make money off of you. Don't fall for it.

What happened yesterday in the stock market won't make you any money. What will happen tomorrow is what counts. So, to keep our eye on the ball, we must not focus on the numbers of buyers and sellers yesterday. We will do much better if we look at what the numbers of *potential* buyers and sellers are telling us is more likely to happen tomorrow.

Sentiment indicators are everywhere, and include

- American Association of Individual Investors (AAII) Sentiment Survey which can be seen at: www.aaii.com/sentimentsurvey. This survey measures individual investor sentiment among members, including those in their investment clubs.

- Adviser and newsletter writer sentiment measures can be seen at the Investor's Intelligence site: www.investorsintelligence.com/x/free_chart.html?r=101l

- Active manager sentiment can be seen at the National Association of Active Investment Managers (NAAIM) website: www.naaim.org/programs/naaim-exposure-index/

Sentiment indicators are only one investment tool. Just like a mechanic will have more than one tool in his or her bag, so do wise investors.

CHAPTER 14 – SELECTING THE RIGHT RESEARCH APPROACH

"The longer one invests the more likely it is that that they will encounter a catastrophic market event. Risk does not go down with time, it goes up!"

John Kenneth Galbraith, noted 20th century economist

There are many ways to do investment research, some horribly complicated and of questionable value. Hopefully, I can shed some light on investment analysis, so you don't waste your life working on something that is not interesting and may become out of date almost immediately. Laziness is the mother of invention, after all.

There are several main schools of investment analysis, among them are **Fundamental, Technical** and **Quantitative** analysis.

Fundamentals look primarily at financial data of the company. **Quantitative** analysis slices and dices the financial data and relies only on the math to identify investment candidates. **Technical** analysis uses charts and graphs to represent investments pictorially. In the next few pages, I will explain the differences in these styles of analysis, so you can decide where to put your attention and what to ignore.

Doing investment analysis can be so overwhelming that few people do decent research even when their life savings are at stake. Most investors become so bogged down that they never learn how to research investments and just go with whatever ads they see, friends they talk to, or information that comes their way, because they literally don't know how to do anything else. It has been said that most people spend more time choosing which refrigerator to buy than choosing investments. This is not an indictment of investors, but a comment on the overwhelming task of sorting through all the data.

Financial advisers, brokers and planners play off this dynamic and appear to know a lot about investments that you don't, and they actually may know more than you. But do they know enough to be considered experts? Much of the time, no. Most are merely salesmen for the mutual funds and annuities their company wants them to push and are not really investment analysts.

It has been said that a little knowledge can be a dangerous thing, and that is rarely truer than when dealing with investments. Individual investors like you don't have to learn it all, but you should protect yourself by making it a point to learn enough about your investments to be able to tell when an adviser is on the right track or not. This book is a good step in that direction.

Intelligent investment selection requires some research, but the amount of data available to be analyzed is way more than any one person can look at, probably more than an army can. Large investment firms that employ teams of fundamental analysts might be able to look at the finances of every publicly traded company, make sense of it all and gain a competitive edge. Most of us are limited to being able to do thorough research on only a handful of companies. This can give our investments a narrow, non-diversified focus and give us a very limited competitive edge when entering the markets.

Understanding the strengths and uses of different forms of analysis can help investors simplify their approach to investing and use tools that make the most sense for them.

USING FUNDAMENTAL ANALYSIS

The biggest part of fundamental analysis involves digging into financial statements. This involves looking at a company's revenue, expenses, assets, liabilities, taxes and all the other financial aspects of a company. Fundamental analysts look at this information to gain insight on what a company's future performance might be. One goal of a fundamental analyst is to estimate the investment value of a stock and its earnings potential versus its speculative value.

Investment value can be determined by cash in the bank or real estate owned by a company. These are hard assets with easy-to-identify values. Other information that can affect a fundamental analysis are company earnings. Are there any? Are they consistent, or does the company lose money in some years? Are earnings rising? Rising faster than other companies?

A consistent stream of dividends also has a value that can be calculated, and dividends can be another risk-reducing aspect of stocks. If you bought shares at $20 and the company paid out $1 of dividends during the year, the amount you had left at risk would be only $19. A year later, only $18 would be at risk, and so on. If dividends are consistent, the value of the dividend can be projected out 5 or 10 years to estimate a company's value in the future.

The real or intrinsic value of a stock can be considered to be the total of its component values. If a $20 stock can be seen to have $15 of real underlying value, then only the amount you pay over the $15 is really at risk. The whole price is not at risk because if the company were sold, you would get back at least the value of its assets as they were liquidated. The top $5 that is at risk in this example is called the speculative value.

Speculative value is the difference between the intrinsic value that can be calculated and the amounts investors pay over that value for the right to own a share of the company. Prices are usually bid up over investment values because investors expect the price of the shares to rise over time as the skill of management working with company assets causes earnings to rise, cash to accumulate, etc.

Prices don't always rise, however, regardless of fundamental values or management efforts, as we find out regularly in the stock markets, and speculative values are the part of the price that is most at risk. The more intrinsic value there is relative to the speculative value, the lower the investment risk. Gauging the relationship of investment value versus speculative value and comparing that to other companies is what fundamental analysis is all about.

Wall Street would have investors believe that a company's financial fundamentals are the only true determinant of value, that the "efficient market" will always be pricing stocks to reflect their real value due to the vast numbers of investors who have access to the data. Therefore, fundamentals should determine how everyone should invest. However, this approach didn't do very well in 2007-09 and cost investors dearly if they were focusing on fundamentals alone.

Like so much that the Wall Street propaganda machine puts out, this advice is based on a smidgen of truth, in this case academic studies covering very long-time periods, often 50, 75 or 100+ years. The results of these studies give the advice gleaned from them a certain trueness and respectability.

Remember, however, the studies that Wall Street is so fond of trotting out are almost always done for pension funds, mutual funds or university endowments that have infinite lives. These studies don't pertain very much to you and I, because we won't live forever. We will need our money in less than 50 or 100 years, maybe in just a few years. These studies misrepresent the investment landscape in which we individual investors operate. In years such as 2007-09, many of our buy-and-hold friends were squashed in a few months and wiped out because they believed the 100-year studies pertained to them. They don't.

And, we must be mindful of the fact that fundamental numbers can be fudged or tweaked with accounting sleight of hand. Some companies, like Lehman Brothers and Enron, cooked the books to make themselves look better on paper than they really were. They both went bankrupt in sudden, spectacular blowups and cost investors billions, with a capital B.

A key issue that I have with fundamental analysis is that you are using last year's data to buy next year's investments, and there are many things affecting your investments that are not going to be factored into fundamental data. Every method of investment analysis has its flaws. Taking a backward-looking approach when investments pay off for forward performance is one of fundamental analysis' flaws.

Another flaw of fundamental analysis is that much of the it is based upon estimates and more estimates estimated on top of earlier estimates. It is like the exercise where one person in a circle whispers a sentence into the ear of their neighbor, who whispers it in the ear of the next person until it gets back around to the beginning. Usually the sentence at the end of the trip bears little resemblance to the one that started the exercise. Estimated values often wander wildly from the truth, too.

The success of fundamental analysis depends upon what happens in the long run, and no one knows what that really means. The long run could be months, years, or even many years before the market recognizes the value a fundamental analyst anticipates. In the meantime, you might want your money, or your investments might run into one of those annoying bear markets that knock almost all investments way down.

Noted economist John Kenneth Galbraith wrote the text book for one of my early college economics classes and is quoted saying, "The longer one invests, the more likely it is that that they will encounter a catastrophic market event. Risk does not go down with time, it goes up!" Investing for the long term serves Wall Street more than you.

PRICE - THE ONLY NUMBER THAT CAN'T BE RIGGED

There is only one number that can't be rigged and that is the price of the shares - the price willing buyers and willing sellers agree to accept in an open market. Don't let Wall Street get you to take your eye off the ball. Price is why we invest, not fundamentals.

Even with accurate numbers, normal earnings comparisons can be very misleading in times of economic change. A stock that looks good based on current earnings might see earnings dry up during a recession or competition from new technologies. Auto companies are notorious for their wild financial cycles, both up and down.

Blindly following fundamentals and assuming markets are so totally efficient that worrying about the price of a stock is irrelevant does not take into account that investors are human, have emotions and frequently act irrationally due to greed or fear, driving prices way above their true value or way below it. Even large fund managers are human and as such can act emotionally.

Fundamental analysis usually is a buy-and-hold investor's favorite tool and they will often say investments should be made only on good fundamental values. If you only consider fundamentals, however, it is like assuming the part of the iceberg you can see is all there is. There is really a lot more going on that other forms of analysis can show us.

IDENTIFY CHANGING MARKETS WITH TECHNICAL ANALYSIS

Please don't get me wrong, fundamentals are an important part of your investment decision making, but they should not be the only part. Keep in mind that the easiest way to reduce risks is to diversify. Looking at different types of data to make investment decisions is another way to diversify, so don't let Wall Street buffalo you into thinking fundamentals are the only thing that matters. In reality, technical analysis and inter-market analysis also matter.

Changing investment environments have much more impact on investors than numbers reported on balance sheets. Dealing with a relentless series of cycles is central to successful investing. That will never change. Bad things happen to good investments if they are held when the market cycles down. All investments cycle. Successful investors expect, prepare for and profit from these cycles. So too should you.

Unless you have 30 or more years to let a generational bear market be worked out by the earnings in a Generational Bull market, buying investments based solely on fundamentals can be a disaster.

Hedge funds can employ groups of PhDs and Nobel Prize winners who crunch numbers and do quantitative analysis, but 90% of the population does not like dealing with numbers, so that leaves most of us out.

One way to deal with the analysis paralysis issue is to focus on just a handful of investments so the data is not so overwhelming. However, what if you don't want to overlook the next Amazon or Google? What if you want to look at all the stocks or mutual funds out there to find those nuggets that you know are waiting for you somewhere? Have you ever wished you had an easy way to sort through a lot of investments? The simple way is to use charts.

Technical analysis is all those charts and graphs that often look like a foreign language to the uninitiated. There is an old saying that a picture is worth a thousand words. Well, a chart is worth a thousand numbers – literally.

As perplexing as charts might seem to novice chart readers, they make investment research a snap compared to poring over financial reports one at a time or endlessly crunching numbers. If you can understand a few words in another spoken language, you can learn to understand charts. I'll show you a few charts and how to use them in a coming chapter.

Since most of us are much more comfortable looking at pictures than doing math, technical analysis is a skill that every investor can benefit from. I'll get into more detail on technical analysis in later chapters but here are some of the basics.

With a picture of what a stock is doing, it is easy to see turning points in the market and know when to buy or sell. Many charting programs or websites will have indicators that can literally flash a signal or send you an email when the stop loss sell parameters that you input are met. Managing your investments doesn't get much easier than that. Knowing your way around charts will give you another tool in your investor tool box, and it is not that difficult to do.

Technical analysis is valuable because only two things make a difference to the markets, as my friend Tom McClellan, publisher of the McClellan Market Report (http://www.mcoscillator.com/), says. Those two things are not fundamentals and not even news, except perhaps over the very short term. What really moves markets is how much money there is and how willing are people to invest it. That is really all there is to it! And only technical analysis can give us insights into these two dynamics.

Some technical analysts, like day traders, think fundamentals are totally irrelevant, so they do nothing but study charts. If you believe in diversification as I do, you know that you probably should mix both technical and fundamental analysis.

Charts have risen to be the leading solution in dealing with investment cycles. Every investor should gain a working knowledge of them to better know when to buy, when to hold, and importantly, when to sell. We will talk more about charts in coming chapters.

The data used most frequently to generate charts is the price of the investment. Nothing fancy, just the price. However, you can put a lot of price data into one line on a chart, and that data can tell us a lot.

There is an art to reading charts and graphs, and, of course, there is never any guarantee that the chart will lead you in the right direction, but you don't have to be perfect to be successful if you couple your investments with protective systems that I describe in coming chapters. Since 1950, the stock market has gone up on only 51% of the days it was open. One easily achievable goal we can have is to improve that probability within our portfolios to something better than 51%. Technical analysis can help you do just that.

Technical analysis can also show us the human side of the markets with its array of charts and graphs. The flow of money and patterns of investment for a particular security, including fear and greed, can't be seen on financial statements, but can be seen on charts. That is where technical analysis becomes truly valuable.

The charts that a technical analyst uses can baffle a newcomer. Just like trying to understand everything your car motor is doing at one time can be a bit overwhelming, trying to understand everything a chart conveys in one glance can be too. If we take one component at a time, however, such as a spark plug, the engine becomes understandable. Charts that look bewildering can be easily understood by looking at the pieces of data represented rather than the whole thing.

When you finish this book, you will be a more well-rounded investor and I'll give you some basics in chart reading to make sure that by using charts you understand the value of confirming investment decisions before investing your money.

PRICE MATTERS MOST

Personally, I don't like to buy anything that is not going up. That rule keeps me out of trouble, away from buying something that the news assures me "is sure to bounce back strongly," and away from the lure of headline grabbing gains to be had by bottom fishing the stock market. I've learned that trying to buy an investment that is still going down is like trying to catch a falling knife. Sometimes you catch it just right, and sometimes you lose a finger.

Before I buy, I like to wait until a stock has bottomed and exhibits a well-defined rise that suggests that the recovery has legs and is more than just a wrinkle in the texture of a continuing decline. That may seem to fly in the face of the "you have to pick price bottoms to time a market" argument because the premise Wall Street presents with this line is flawed. No one can know that a price bottom is in until after the fact and prices have started to rise. I may pay a higher price waiting for confirmations that the bottom is behind me and not still ahead, but *my goal is really to buy high and sell higher,* not buy low and sell high, period. That is an unrealistic goal.

This muddying of the water around proactive investing is part of the "market timer" labeling that Wall Street uses to prejudice the average investor against ever being a proactive investor and moving out of the market. It's just another facet of the relentless PR attack Wall Street employs to get those of us here on Main Street to make wrong moves.

Trying to pick absolute bottoms or tops in a market is a fool's game. No one can know if a price top is the final top until prices enter a well-defined downtrend. If someone tells you they know with certainty that a top or bottom is happening right then, put your hand on your wallet and back slowly out of the room, because you are talking to a snake oil salesman. I let the market tell me when the bottom has occurred and that takes some time.

COMBINE TYPES OF ANALYSIS TO CREATE ROBUST PORTFOLIOS

My method of investing is fairly systematic. To create effective diversification, I use several types of analyses:

1.   **Inter-market Analysis:** I measure the gains of broad indexes to determine the strength of various markets such as stocks vs. bonds, U.S. stocks vs. foreign stocks, small company stocks vs. large company stocks, value stocks vs. growth stocks, etc. In the 2000-03 bear market, value stocks were the strongest market segment. Knowing these

relationships helps me put more money into stronger markets and less into weaker ones.

2. **Quantitative Analysis:** I use a proprietary Quality of Trend Analysis that I have developed over the years to evaluate and grade the upward momentum of investments. Specifically, I am looking for stocks with the smallest declines relative to their upward momentum. This mathematical process identifies stocks that the hedge funds, pension funds and mutual funds are buying. It allows me to boil down thousands of stocks into a short list of possible stocks that I know are attracting a lot of other buyers. Lots of buyers for your investment are always a good thing.

3. Next, I do a **fundamental analysis** of the 30-50 stocks that are at the top of the list in my Quality of Trend Analysis to be sure that the companies with good momentum also have good earnings, are not drowning in debt, etc. This helps pare down 30-50 stocks to perhaps only 10 or 15.

4. In the final step, I look at the charts for each investment still on the short list to see how many look like they are at obvious buy-points and it is a good time to buy. This is pure **technical analysis**, during which I can also see the personality of this investment, such as

- Does it drop sharply and rise sharply?
- Does it look good due to a one-time event?
- Do the up/down cycles have any regularity to them?
- Are there certain times, such as at earnings releases, when the price becomes more volatile?

All of these characteristics can be seen on charts and can give you insights as to what to expect from a stock. Charts can also show me where I will want to sell this investment if it doesn't work out as planned.

Using all four of these broad styles of analysis is like having four legs on a "portfolio stool." It gives my portfolios a robustness that many portfolios lack if they use only one primary method of investment selection.

If you are not familiar with the term robust, it is used in the investment world to identify strategies that can weather more types of markets than something less robust. If you plan to invest in both up markets and down markets, a robust strategy will be one that can serve you well in both environments. Many managers use only a one-trick pony whose strategies do well when markets roar ahead but get hammered hard when they decline. Those are not robust strategies.

The reason I focus so much on the charts and the numbers that generate them is that all of the information that can be known about a freely traded investment, including the consensus of what millions of investors think will happen in the future, is distilled into one single number, the price of the investment.

The price tells it all. It can't be faked, and it is not fuzzy. Everything else is a distraction. That is why price is the basis of most of the charts I use. And if the price action tells me that the sum total of all investors is saying "forget fundamentals. It is time to get out of this investment," I'll get out, too.

Don't worry about making a mistake with your investment analysis. We don't have to be right all of the time, in fact we can't. We just have to have some tools to recognize when we are wrong and minimize the damage, and to recognize when we are right - so we can maximize the gains when we are right - and tell us to make adjustments when we are in high-risk times. With these steps, we can keep our losses smaller than our gains and keep more of our money.

One doesn't need to be perfectly good to be great. A 2007 analysis of the mutual fund performance of the 1,228 equity funds listed in the Morningstar database, which at that time had 15-year track records, shows what it takes to be at the top of your peer group. Only 198, or 16%, of all mutual fund managers were in the top half of their class each year. If your investment returns are only above average every year you could be in the top 1/6th of all investors. Above average is not so difficult to achieve, but it does eliminate index funds from consideration if that is your goal, because index funds just shoot for average.

If being in the top 1/6th of all investors still leaves you with an underachiever complex, shoot for the top 1/3 of your class every year and you may end up in the top 7% of all investors. The top 3% of the group of all managers merely had to be in the top 1/4 of their peer groups.

Look at how many investors settle for index fund investing, which guarantees something like average returns. I say *something like average* because true index funds have expenses that almost always draw their returns below the actual index they are tracking, meaning below average. Index funds that produce above index returns are straying and taking some extra risk along the way somewhere. For most of us, consistent returns that keep us somewhere above average is a more practical, more realistic and more effective goal than trying to shoot the lights out with your investments – or just trying to be average.

The message that proactive investors understand is that technical analysis tries to get more consistent gains than can be achieved from passive buy-and-hope-it-works-out investing that often is accompanied by so many devastating losses. We understand that the American investment creed of buy low, sell high has two parts and one has to be ready to sell at some point to achieve the goal. We are not greedy market timers trying to pick exact market tops and bottoms as Wall Street tries to paint anyone who advocates selling. We just want to manage and reduce the risks that all investors face, so we can have more money invested when markets are going up and less invested when markets are going down. That is the simplest way to investment success.

Fundamental analysis investors who cling to investments in declining markets are like the Red Coats of the Revolutionary War. They had a way of doing things that could be very effective in the right environment, but they refused to adapt to obvious changes in the circumstances and got whipped by a small, poorly equipped group of rebels that had the good sense to change tactics during each battle. Do you have the good sense to change when things around you change?

Investment managers who are willing to adapt to changes in the markets seem to have an inherent advantage in this rapidly changing investment environment. Think of us as the Minutemen of this industry.

CHAPTER 15 - USING TECHNICAL INDICATORS

"Anyone who says you cannot time a market just doesn't know how to do it."

Will Hepburn

Technical analysis indicators, typically in the form of a chart, are used to alert us that the market is changing, and some action might be warranted.

Let's look at some simple technical analysis tools that can tell you what investments to buy, when to buy them, and when to sell. These are basic tools that you can learn to use right now without being a math whiz or an MBA.

Technical analysis primarily uses just three pieces of data for each day or time period being studied. The most widely used is **price data** and we will devote our time here to price charts. The other two, **volume**, meaning the number of shares being traded, and **breadth** indicators which are based upon the numbers of rising or falling stocks, are topics for another book.

One big issue when using charts is deciding on what time horizon you want to use. The market can be going down in the short term, but up in the long term, so which is correct? Both are correct, but the question should be "which is more significant to you?"

Short-term indicators can tell you to get in or out of a market after only a very short move on the stock's or index's part. This can be very helpful when trying to manage the risk of a market decline. Short-term indicators will have you out of the market with a very small loss, but you will also get a lot of signals, often more than investors want to deal with, and often many small losses to go with them.

Longer-term indicators, which can take months to develop signals, will generate fewer signals so they can more easily be used within 401ks or fund families that restrict the number of trades you can place. Longer-term indicators are best used by investors who don't care about short-term gyrations in the market and only want to avoid the longest declines, which also tend to be the largest declines. The problem with longer-term indicators is that in the months that some systems take to generate sell signals, the market can drop considerably.

To be a successful investor you need to understand your comfort level with these different holding periods, weighing your interest in watching the markets versus protecting your investments from a market decline. The time frames most commonly used in technical indicators are:

- ◆ **Day Trading** involves frequent trading with minute to minute data, called real time data, versus the end-of-day data that we see posted in the *Wall Street Journal* or *Investor's Business Daily*. Most day traders sell all of their holdings at the end of each day, so they can sleep without worrying about their stocks overnight. In other words, kids don't try this at home.

- ◆ **Short-Term Trading** involves holding periods in the days to weeks range and is usually only done by very experienced or professional stock traders who watch the market all day and want to get in, make a small profit in a few days and get out. Short-term traders watching multiple investments can generate a huge number of trades.

- ◆ **Intermediate-Term Trading** is where holding periods are measured in weeks to months. This is the type of trading I prefer, because I feel it is the best blend of risk control with indicators that will have me out of market declines very early, but also give room for my winners to run. I am also willing to look at the market every day to tend my garden of stocks and do some weeding if necessary. Intermediate-term trading frees one up from having their face glued to a computer monitor all day, but still allows one to have a finger on the pulse of the market. This type of trading will have average holding periods of less than one year, so will generate a fair number of trades. My current portfolio holds 23 stocks with a nine-month average holding period. If you are willing to watch your investments daily or at a minimum, weekly, this may be a good time frame for you to focus on. Only some of the gains achieved using an intermediate time frame are long-term capital gains, but even owning mutual funds can generate a lot of short-term gains.

♦ **Long-Term Investing** is the type Warren Buffett does, where he intends to hold every investment he buys forever. Being an optimist and having confidence in your investment selection helps generate this kind of attitude, but some realism needs to be there too. If an investment is not working, Warren Buffett culls it from his portfolio, and he has tools to tell him when he is wrong. His holding period is measured in years, but there have been many holdings sold after shorter periods because they were losing money. Even Warren Buffett doesn't get it right all of the time.

Many long-term investors only look at their investments monthly or quarterly and trade only in long-term declines. This is a very doable style of investing for most individual investors.

♦ **Buy-and-Hold** is the type of investing advocated by most brokers, financial planners and investment advisers with FINRA licenses due to the restrictions they face when moving money around for their clients. Few will have any system to tell you when to sell an investment other than when the red ink has been flowing onto your statements and you complain. Buy-and-hold is simple to understand, easy to implement and half the time works out well. The other half of the time, not so well....

Since all big declines begin as small ones, I respect all declines, and for that reason have settled into the Intermediate-term camp so I usually have my clients out of markets early in declines. However, I also have very low trading costs, and the more you trade, the more these costs matter.

I hope that you will take a few minutes to reflect on these trading time frames and find which one you fit into. In my examples that follow, I use daily pricing in my charts because I think it serves the most non-professional investors.

Really, all we are trying to do with any indicator is to notice when the market or an individual stock turns around and does something different from what it had been doing previously, giving us an opportunity to react to the change, if warranted. Proactive management is much more about avoiding risk than hitting home runs with investments. The real goal is identifying up trends and down trends so that we can participate or retreat to a safe haven when losses are likely.

UNDERSTANDING AND USING TRENDLINES

The most basic definition of an uptrend is a series of rising prices in a security. If both the tops and bottoms in the zigzag of a price chart are rising you have a pretty clear uptrend. Likewise, declines are marked by a number of falling tops and falling bottoms as the texture of the chart evolves. Trends can be more easily seen with the use of trendlines drawn across price tops in falling markets and bottoms in rising markets.

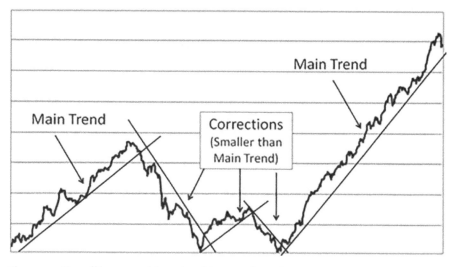

Figure 9 - Trendlines provide a visual image of market movements.

Top and bottom trendlines are used in this manner for good reasons. A trendline drawn across the bottoms of a trend indicates levels of "support," meaning the buyers who are watching this security think these are the prices at which the security is attractive. When these prices are reached, they begin to buy in large enough numbers to keep the stock price from declining through the line of the trend. When prices drop below the line, the uptrend may be broken. This is called a breakdown in prices and is a negative indicator.

As humans, we tend to think that at any one moment we are the only one looking at a particular stock. However, there are many millions of investors worldwide who may be interested in buying the same stock you are. Remembering this allows the idea of large groups of investors watching for particular prices to make sense.

Similar to support, a trendline drawn across the tops of a price line mark levels of "resistance," which are prices at which enough of the buyers may decide that a price is too high for them. Rather than buying, they may sell a little bit or just watch, but they stop buying. That is enough to shift the balance of buyers and sellers and move prices downward. When bargain hunting buyers are attracted in numbers large enough to move the stock price up, the price line will break out above the trendline. This is called a price breakout and is a bullish indicator.

Trendlines are visual representations of supply and demand in the market. Top and bottom trendlines can be used at the same time if one wishes to see both support and resistance because both work to define a trend regardless of the direction.

REDUCING CHART NOISE

There can be a lot of sharp movements up and down in a price chart that can easily confuse us in the heat of the moment. Sharp movements

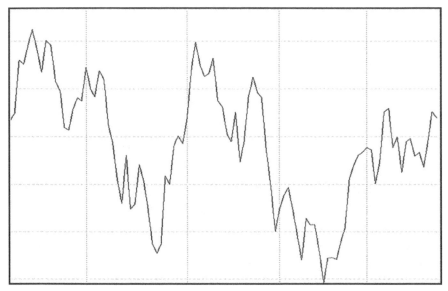

Figure 10 - Market volatility can result in noisy price charts where trends are hard to observe.

that obscure the message a chart can deliver are called noise. Let me show you how to deal with noise in a chart.

This is a noisy price chart. It is hard to tell where the trend is with this security. After all, the ending price on the right side of the chart is just where it began on the left side of the chart. If we want to see through noise in the market, we can use an easy-to-understand indicator called a moving average.

Moving averages are just averages of the most recent past prices. A 21-day moving average is common because there are about 21 trading days in a calendar month. Depending on how the calendar falls, there could be more or less than 21 trading days, but 21 is a good average. So, a 21-day average looks back at a month's worth of prices adding the 21 prices and then dividing by 21. The average is recalculated each day to add the most recent day and drop the oldest day from the data. For this reason, the indicator is said to move with the current day's pricing, hence the name moving average.

Day traders may calculate moving averages by the minute. For very long-term analysis, monthly closing prices may be used. For our purposes in this book, we will be using daily closing prices and more commonly used time periods such as 21 days, 50 days or 200 days.

Each investment has its own personality, and some perform better with the use of different time periods, so 21, 50 and 200 days may not work for every investment.

By adding a 21-day moving average of prices to this same price chart it becomes a smoother line. Suddenly, the trend is easy to see.

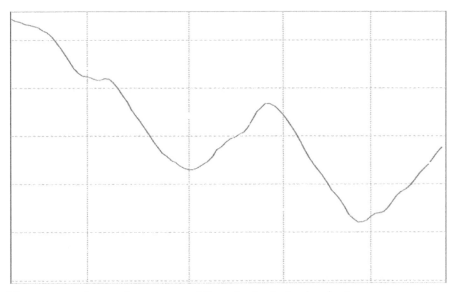

Figure 11 - 21 day moving average of the prior "noisy" price chart.

On the next page, the price chart has the moving average overlaying the price to make the relationship easier to see. The 21-day moving average clearly shows that the overall momentum is down, although it is turning up at the end.

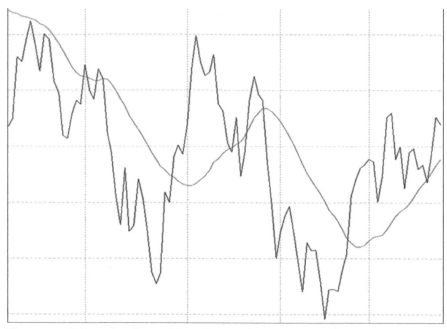

Figure 12 - Noisy price chart with 21-day moving average overlay.

Moving averages can do more than remove noise from a chart, they can also give us buy and sell signals to get us in or out of a market in a timely manner. How would you like a system that would have had you out of the stock market in 2008? Here's one that worked.

USING MOVING AVERAGES TO GENERATE BUY AND SELL SIGNALS

Let's start with a price chart showing daily closing prices for the S&P 500 Index, generally considered representative of the whole stock market. I use the S&P 500 for this work because it represents about 80% of all dollars invested in U.S. stocks. The Dow Jones Industrials Index, with only 30 stocks, represents only 1/4 of all investment dollars, so I feel the S&P 500 is more representative of the market as a whole, even if the Dow makes all the headlines.

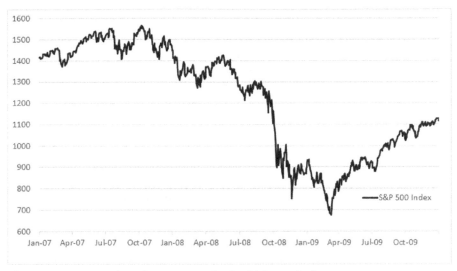

Figure 13 - Bear market of 2007-2009 in the S&P 500 Index.

This chart shows the worst bear market of the past 75 years, the 2007-09 decline, which included a 56% loss in value to the index and funds that tracked the index. It is easy to see that 2008 would have been a good time to be out of the stock market, but how does one know exactly when to get out and when to get back in? Just trying to pick spots to sell or buy based upon the news or how you feel about the world is usually a bad system.

A simple buy/sell indicator can be made by averaging the past prices of the stock or index we are focused upon and looking at the current price to see if it is above or below the average. This is called a moving average indicator. An average of the last 200 days closing prices is a common long-term indicator that changes very slowly as the indicator is recalculated each day.

Figure 14 - A 200-day moving average is added to the 2007-2009 S&P 500

Applying a 200-day moving average to our S&P 500 chart allows us to see the smoothing action it applies to the price history from which it is created. The 200-day moving average makes it easy to tell when the downturn is really underway and when it has ended. Buy and sell signals are generated when the daily price line crosses the moving average line.

But what about those many instances where the noisy daily price poked above or below the moving average only to move back a short time later in what we call a false signal or failed signal? Noisy prices can generate a lot of false signals. If we had bought or sold at every moving average crossing, we would have generated a lot more trades than we might have wanted and cut into our profit.

A simple solution to this problem is to pair up two moving averages, a faster one, which uses fewer days in the calculation, will change direction more quickly than the longer moving average, but still smooths the price action to reduce the number of false signals. A 50-day moving average is often paired with the 200-day moving average for this purpose.

Figure 15 - Paired 50-day and 200-day moving averages of the S&P 500 generate the Death Cross and Golden Cross signals.

This moving average crossover technique gave us much clearer signals, and in this three-year period only generated two trades, one sell and one buy. The sell was triggered by the 50-day average moving below the 200-day moving average on January 8, 2008, a signal called a "Death Cross." Since this indicator uses closing prices, you would not have known about the crossover until after the market closed that day, so you would have been able to exit the market on January 9, 2008. The buy signal came on August 12, 2009, when the 50-day moving average crossed above the 200-day average, in what is known as a "Golden Cross."

Would this strategy have been good enough to save you a lot of angst, lost money or postponed retirement plans? I'm guessing so.

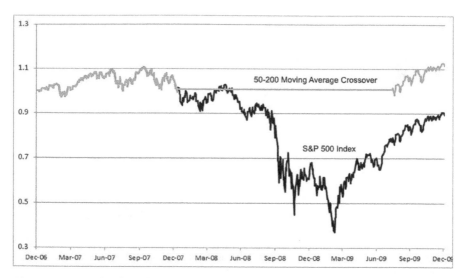

Figure 16 - Result of combining 50- and 200-day moving averages to generate buy and sell signals.

Some people will say that these simple indicators lag the market so much as to make them undesirable, but our example of using 50- and 200-day moving average crossover signals reduced our loss to only 11% from the 2007 high before exiting the market on January 9, 2008. Considering that the market declined by more than half after our exit, I'd call that a timely move. When your risk ends up being 1/5 of that which an index fund buy-and-hold investor experiences, that is a very good thing and demonstrates why I am an advocate of proactive management.

Lay your hand over the right side of this chart so that only data up to January 10, 2008 is showing. Would you have known to get out of the market at this point without a system like this, a system that would tell you it was time to forget growth and preserve capital? Few investors did and they paid steep prices later in 2008 when the market dropped another 50% after our signal.

There! With this one tip, this book may have just paid for itself many times over. Please tell your friends!

INVESTORS WHO LOSE THE LEAST END UP WITH THE MOST

As I mentioned earlier, these systems may not be perfect, but in really nasty markets, everyone will lose something. Investors who lose the least will end up with the most because they have more money to reinvest when the markets do recover. Someone following this 50- and 200-day moving average crossover indicator and sitting out the bear market in cash would have re-entered the market with around 90% of their capital intact on August 12, 2009, just a few months after the market bottomed in March of that year. Buy-and-hold investors who rode the market all the way to the bottom and back up would have had only 67% of their investment capital working for them by the reentry date and no extra cushion from interest collected while in cash.

Over the three-year period from December 31, 2006 to December 31, 2009, the S&P 500 closing price first rose, then bottomed and recovered a bit creating a net decline of 21.38%, or an average of 7.70% lost per year over the three-year period (performance data from FastTrack). Following the signals from your 50-day and 200-day moving average crossover system would have generated a gain of over 10.15%, an average 3.37% per year. That is a difference of 11.07% per year, with our simple timing system soundly beating the index. Anyone who says you cannot time a market just doesn't know how to do it. Show them this simple system and see what they say.

Some folks call a buy signal issued by this 50x200-day crossover the Golden Cross. Maybe now you understand why.

Not all investments can be managed well with our 50-day and 200-day moving average crossover system because each investment moves up and down differently. Also, this same system will give different results, perhaps causing losses, when applied over different time frames than shown here.

There is both an art and a science to investment analysis. Developing these indicators is the science of technical analysis. Determining which indicator to use when, and what time frames to apply them to is the art of technical analysis. Fundamental analysis has only so much science in it and applying that science is very artful and very subjective. Technical analysis shares this trait too.

Just as buying a shiny new box full of tools at Sears won't make you a good mechanic, knowing about a few indicators won't complete the job of making you a skilled technical analyst. The mechanic needs to know which tool to use in which situation and whether to turn the wrench right or left. In this same way, you will need practice to see your indicator give a signal and recognize that signal for what it is. Then, of course, you have to act on it. Don't worry about making mistakes. Even skilled technical analysts make mistakes. We just have ways to identify mistakes early and correct them, as I discuss in coming chapters.

My purpose in presenting these insights into technical analysis is not to make you an expert money manager. There are many more indicators that can be applied, and a lot of practice required before you become proficient at reading charts. However, I do want to pique your interest enough for you to perhaps learn more about technical analysis, so you can use it along with your other investment knowledge.

There are many free charting websites along with tutorials on YouTube. Some top free charting programs include StockCharts.com, Yahoo Finance, Google, BigCharts.com, and FreeStockCharts.com.

In 2000, I was asked to address the state convention of AAII, the American Association of Individual Investors, which helps organize and train so many local investment clubs. At that time, the AAII was a staunch proponent of buy-and-hold investing as the only viable system for its members because buy-and-hold had worked well for the previous 18 years. The bear market of 2000-03 was just beginning to unfold, so in my talk I suggested that reducing exposure to the stock market by selling investments was one of the best ways to deal with the decline everyone had begun to notice. I was treated like a blasphemer and shunned by all but a handful of those in attendance.

I find it just a little ironic that AAII now promotes technical analysis and has extensive resource lists showing what to look for in a charting program on their website, AAII.com. Check it out, too.

At least we know that the mainstream is finally accepting technical analysis for the great tool that it is.

CHAPTER 16 - HEDGING AWAY MARKET RISK

"Technical analysis is a windsock, not a crystal ball. Be prepared to adjust your tactics if conditions change."

Carl Swenlin, Founder, DecisionPoint.com

The technology-based explosion of financial vehicles has created a variety of new securities one can use to invest, including mutual funds, and more lately Exchange Traded Funds, commonly called ETFs. One variety of these funds that has particular use in reducing risk is the short or inverse fund.

Inverse funds are generally linked to an index and are calculated to perform exactly opposite of the index itself. If you want to reduce the risk of being invested without having to sell your favorite holdings, inverse funds can be a great tool to let you have your cake and eat it too.

Some refer to this tactic as shorting a market, but that implies an all or nothing bet against a stock or a market. Rarely is the market environment so black and white as to invite an all or nothing bet. However, I will occasionally use the term "short" to describe an inverse fund or ETF just because that is a term accepted in the industry and old habits die hard.

Pairing up investments that move opposite to one another to preserve values is called hedging, a tactic first developed by farmers to protect themselves from fluctuations in crop prices before the end of the growing season.

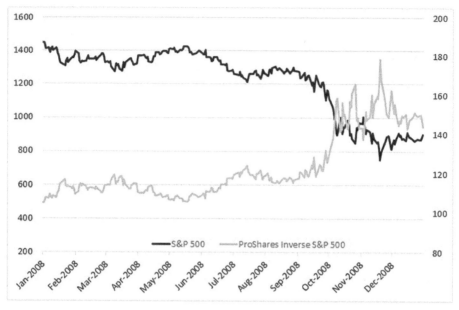

Figure 17 – S&P 500 index fund versus S&P 500 short fund.

As you can see from the chart, when the index moves up the inverse fund moves down. They are mirror images of each other. No one in their right mind would buy 50% of the index and 50% of the inverse fund because the average of the two would be close to zero, and there is no point in investing to gain zero.

By pairing a strong investment with an inverse fund based upon a weaker index, we can get some interesting results. The key is to use similar investments whose price movements stay correlated, meaning they move at the same time even if one moves up and the other down. Pairing investments whose prices are not closely correlated, such as gold and the S&P 500 index, usually doesn't work very well.

Let us look at an example of a fun way to reduce the risk of investing in the stock market by owning the strongest and hedging against the weakest market segment. If the S&P 500 Index, which is mostly large company stocks, is stronger than the Total Stock Market Index, it makes sense to assume that the S&P 500 might be down less than the broad market during a down cycle in the market. And if the Russell 2000 index of small company stocks is one of the weaker parts of the overall market, it is safe to assume that it will be down more than the Total Stock Market Index.

At the risk of throwing so many numbers at you that your eyes may roll back in your head I am going to explain what happens when you use this approach. You can skip to the chart, below, if you wish, and this explanation may make more sense to you if you come back to it.

Let's assume:

- Total Stock Market Index representing the average drops 10%,
- S&P 500 fund we use goes down only 7.5% because it is stronger than the average,
- Russell 2000 fund goes down 12.5%, because it is weaker than average.

If our portfolio was invested half in the S&P 500 fund and hedged with half in an inverse of the Russell 2000 fund, we would:

- Lose 7.5% on the 50% invested in the S&P 500 fund,
- Gain 12.5% on the Inverse Russell 2000 fund
- Net 2.5% (5% gain on half of our money)

We also offset our market risk because if one fund goes down, the other should go up, greatly smoothing the combined holdings.

We can do just as well in a rising market because if the market moves up one fund will gain value as the other fund goes down. In this example let's assume:

- Total Stock Market Index representing the average goes up 10%,
- S&P 500 fund we use goes up 12.5% because it is stronger than the average,
- Russell 2000 fund goes down 7.5%, because it is weaker than average.

Again, with a 50/50 portfolio, we would:

- Lose 7.5% on the 50% invested in the weaker Inverse Russell 2000 fund,
- Gain 12.5% on the S&P 500 fund
- Net 2.5% (5% gain on half of our money)

Since a chart is worth 1,000 numbers, let's see how this example works in pictures.

In early 2009, the stock markets were still in a pretty steep decline. These charts look at what one can do to make money in a falling market, using a technology index fund (RYTIX, Rydex Technology Fund) between December 31, 2008 and March 9, 2009.

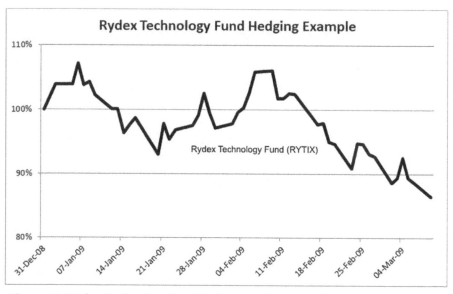

Figure 18 - Rydex Technology Fund from December 2008 through March 2009.

As you can see on the chart above, the tech fund lost 13.93% of its value in a little over three months. As bad as that was, the tech sector was one of the strongest at the time. The S&P 500 was much weaker in comparison, losing over 30% of its value during that same period.

In the charts below, we pair 50% of an inverse of the weaker S&P

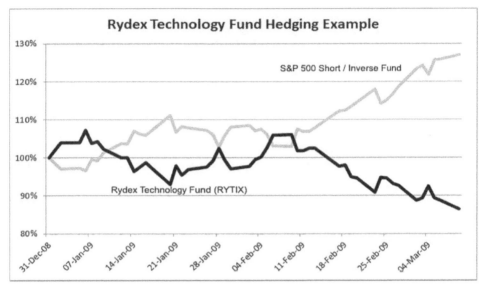

Figure 20 - Rydex Technology Fund contrasted with an S&P 500 short position.

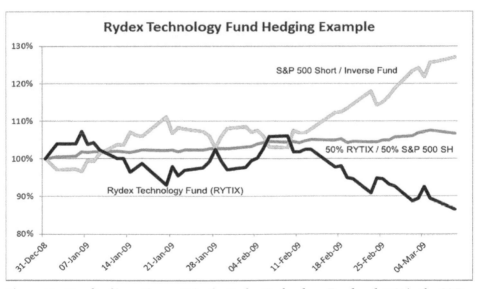

Figure 19 - Result of investing 50% in the Rydex Technology Fund and 50% in the S&P 500 short position.

500 fund with 50% of the stronger tech fund.

When we average these two price lines together, we have a gain for this trade in the 7% range. But significantly, as you can see in the preceding chart, this gain is made with almost no volatility in your account value even though the market around you was crashing.

This tactic is particularly useful if you have some favorite holdings, perhaps with large gains, that you would prefer to hold onto rather than sell and trigger taxes on those gains.

In my portfolios, I have noticed that weaker stocks normally trigger stop loss levels before stronger stocks. (Chapter 17 looks at using stop losses in greater detail.) In times of general market weakness, as weaker stocks trigger stop-loss levels and are sold, I will often use some of that cash to add a hedge to offset the risk of continuing to hold my stronger positions.

In this way, my portfolios evolve to stay in sync with the markets while effectively managing the risk of being invested. This also keeps me from making all or nothing bets on the stock market, a tactic that can go wrong with expensive results. By using this technique, your portfolios can stay in tune with what is really happening in the markets and you can experience more consistent returns.

As a disclosure, these inverse relationships are much easier to see in hindsight than they are in day-to-day business. The longer trends continue, the easier they become to identify and use compared with short trends. This is the type of tactic you can develop when you have become an experienced chart reader.

And as Carl Swenlin, Founder of DecisionPoint.com, now a part of StockCharts.com has said, "***Technical analysis is a windsock, not a crystal ball.*** Be prepared to adjust your tactics if conditions change."

CHAPTER 17 - STOPS - THE EASIEST WAY TO BE A GOOD INVESTOR

" . . . holding losing investments is a loser's game! That may seem to be a harsh way to phrase that aphorism, but sometimes investors need a slap in the face or they might end up with a slap in the wallet."

Will Hepburn

Some aspects of investing are simple, timeless, and apply in all kinds of markets. One constant is that holding losing investments is a loser's game! That may seem to be a harsh way to phrase that aphorism, but sometimes investors need a slap in the face or they might end up with a slap in the wallet.

Wall Street's rules of thumb often sound good but eventually work against the average investor and in the favor of Wall Street. Now, you may not consider yourself to be average, but if you have ever owned an index fund you are settling for average returns. If you have ever waited for an investment to get back to breakeven before selling, then this chapter can help you pay for this book many times over.

Many stock brokers after selling you a stock that goes down will say something to the effect of *"If you loved XYZ at $50, you must really love it at $40!"* They then add the rationale that by buying more at $40, the price will lower your breakeven point to $45, the average price of your $40 and $50 purchases. This tactic is called averaging down. They forget that your goal should not be just to break even, but to make profits. If the price falls even further, you will likely be advised to protect your investment. Buy more! *"Average your buy price down and your breakeven point will be even lower,"* common advice says. It kind of makes sense, until you realize the premise is flawed.

Please repeat after me: Buying losing investments is a loser's game!

Legendary investor and founder of *Investor's Business Daily*, William O'Neil, teaches anyone who will listen to never hold a stock that drops by 8%. Sell it right away! You can always buy it back if the stock recovers, but no one ever knows just how far a stock will fall before it recovers, especially the stock brokers who, after all, are primarily stock salesmen, not stock analysts.

I don't know if an 8% loss is the right level to sell a declining position or how O'Neil chose that particular number because each investment has its own personality. Any one investment will act one way in up markets and differently in down markets. I'm guessing that 8% was his average number and he needed a single number for investors to focus upon.

However, O'Neil's point is a good one. Don't hold losers! Cull them from your portfolios and be ruthless about it.

Many investors, and many advisers too, get ego involved in their investments. If you select an investment, I'm guessing you are proud of your work, your insight and your astute analysis, even if it only extended to counting Morningstar stars on your mutual fund selection. Sometimes it is hard to admit that your choice is not working out, but it's a fact that many investments don't work out, for you or for professionals like myself. The difference between how a professional acts and a less experienced investor is that the pro will know that when bad things happen to good investments because the markets have changed, they have to change too. They have to adapt or they will lose their job to someone who can.

When a professional manager buys an investment, he will already know at what point he will change his mind about its desirability and sell the investment. A point at which you will sell an investment that turns around is called a "stop loss" price. There are many ways to calculate stops, as they are called in the business, and stop prices can change as an investment matures **but the most important thing about stops is to have one.**

The reason that this is so important is that a predetermined stop takes the emotion out of the decision to sell. You don't have to agonize over the decision, you have already decided that this was the price to sell at. You eliminate the ego argument that your investment is a good one or you wouldn't have bought it in the first place and the market will recognize this soon. This common mind trap keeps many investors holding losers long after they should have been sold, making losses much deeper than they could have been.

The biggest single mistake I see investors make is to wait for an investment to reach breakeven before selling. This is another ego-fueled problem because no one likes to take a loss. Many investments never, ever get back to where they once were, leaving investors holding losers for years, sometimes forever.

The real question to ask yourself in this situation is "how much money is my investment worth today, and is this the best spot for my money to be? If your original investment is going down, almost any other place will be better. Repeat after me, **"Don't hold losers!"**

If you have a stock with which you have an emotional attachment, such as stock you inherited or stock of the company at which you work or have worked, it is often difficult to make the right decisions about it. Emotional attachments can be one of the largest obstacles to building a better portfolio. It is called familiarity bias and causes you to think differently about that investment than you do about your other stocks.

Let's say you have $300,000 of stock in a good old company. One way to think clearly about the investment is to say to yourself, **"I have $300,000 in cash. Do I want to put this whole amount into this one stock today?"** If the answer is no, it is probably time to develop an exit strategy for the holding and at least pare the amount back so that you have reasonable diversification and protect yourself from a lightning-strike occurrence at your company.

Often tax liability can cloud this decision, but if you find yourself in this position, I would suggest you focus on the portion you get to keep after taxes rather than the tax itself. Preserving 85% of your money sounds much better than paying 15% tax on some gain. Don't let the tax tail wag the dog.

It is much easier to make money investing by keeping more money in investments that are going up and less in investments that are going down. Will Rogers had it right when he said **"Don't gamble; take all your savings and buy some good stock and hold it till it goes up, then sell it. If it don't go up, don't buy it."**

To accomplish Roger's advice, I advocate a modified buy-and-hold technique. Only buy investments that are going up and continue to hold them only as long as they go up. If they stop going up, sell. Repeat as necessary. It's simple really, just not easy to do without some systems to guide you!

If you take an airplane ride to Hawaii, the pilot doesn't just point the plane toward the Islands and forget about it. He has instruments to tell him when to adjust his course left or right, up or down. A stop loss is one of the best instruments to keep your investments on course. And they don't cost a thing!

Many investors will hold onto losers because they are frozen into inaction, sometimes called the "paralysis of analysis." Sometimes it is ego based, such as wanting to avoid taking a loss. After all, the Wall Street saying is that it is not really a loss until you sell. Hooey! A loss is a loss regardless of where it occurs.

AVERAGE UP, NOT DOWN

If averaging down on stock purchases is the wrong way to do things, averaging up must be the right way, right? Right. Actually, averaging up is a much better risk control tactic than averaging down is, and is a tactic used by many professional managers to reduce the risk of entering an investment and having it turn down.

For example, let's assume that you want to build a portfolio of stocks and you decide to buy the stock of XYZ company. A common risk is to have XYZ turn down before you have a significant gain that protects your original capital. Frankly, none of us, even the pros, have crystal balls and can tell when a correction is going to send even good stock prices down. So, you need to protect yourself from this common occurrence by using a stop loss price, say 8% below your buy price, and averaging into the full position you want to hold in this stock.

To average in, you initially buy only 1/3 of your target allocation. Don't buy any more XYZ until you have a 3-5% profit in the holding and then buy another 1/3 of your allocation goal. When you get another 3-5% profit, buy enough XYZ to get to your full allocation.

If XYZ stops rising after your initial buy you only have a small amount at risk. If XYZ has gone up enough that you have become fully invested, you already have a nice gain, so if it then goes down and triggers your stop, you have cushioned any loss with the 6-10% profits required before investing all of your money.

PROTECT YOUR GAINS BY ADJUSTING STOPS

If you follow the advice William O'Neil gives in *Investor's Business Daily* to always have an 8% maximum stop loss on any investment and you average yourself into a holding as I just suggested, you have the comfort of knowing that you have a roughly 8% gain in your XYZ before you are fully invested, reducing your risk to a very small number. After that, you are playing with *house money* and your original savings is no longer at risk. Smart, yes?

Another simple tactic to use in times of general market unrest, political or global instability, or negative news about your investment is to rely on your stops. Do not sell in an emotional response to the news. Make sure your stops move up as the price of your investments rise. If you are particularly nervous or have a large gain to protect, tighten your stops. Instead of using a standard number such as IBD's 8% stop, make it 5% or 4%. You will be out of the market quicker than with the larger stops and give back less of your profits before exiting the position. Tight stops make you more vulnerable to being sold out of rising investments during temporary market dips, but if it will help you sleep better, do it. Tighten your stops.

A bad tactic that many investors use is to sell big winners, often because of some advice in the media about the market being so high. *"You never go broke taking profits"* is the old Wall Street adage. However, as I said earlier, Wall Street rules of thumb usually favor Wall Street, not you. In this case, it gives a pro a chance to pick up shares in a strong stock, something they always love to do.

The correct advice is to *sell your losers and let your winners run.*

If you have winning investments and you don't want to see your gains evaporate, just set a stop loss price and tighten it if you are especially nervous. Don't sell the investment while it is going up, because chances are that a stock on a strong run will continue up. Only sell when it turns down and hits your stop. Don't try to act like you have a crystal ball. You don't. Just use this proven technique and have a stop on each of your investments.

Brokerage firms can have their computers track your holdings and when the market reaches your stop loss price, a change is triggered to create an open sell order for your shares. If you want the freedom and convenience of not having to watch your investments closely, computerized stops are a great tool.

Stop loss orders can be set at a specific price, such as *if my $10 stock drops to $9, sell,* limiting your risk to around 10% of your purchase price. Specific price orders like this need to be monitored and updated if the stock price rises and moves away from your original stop. If the stock price rises to $12, the original $9 stop leaves you with a $3 or 25% potential loss. If you want to limit your potential loss to 10%, you need to move the stop loss price to 90% of its current $12 price, or up to $10.80.

Stops can also be set at a specific percentage below the highest price. These are called **trailing stops** because they stay at a certain distance below the highest price, following it up, but not down. They don't need as much of your attention as prices rise, so percentage stops are convenient. In our example, a 10% stop would automatically move to $10.80 when the price first hit $12.

Parabolic stops will tighten the spread between the highest price and the stop loss price so that big gains end up with tighter stops. Stops can also be combined with limit orders, but getting into the minutiae of order types is beyond the scope of this book. I just want to make you aware that there are a wide variety of order types that can make proactive management easier to implement. Ask your account custodian for a list of order types they can help you with.

Personally, I don't use computerized stops because I want the ability to decide if the stock is in a true decline or if some temporary news has driven the price down. Even good earnings reports can trigger a wave of selling in go-go growth stocks, triggering stop loss orders. Frequently these sharp sell offs are met with another wave of buying and the stock rebounds, frustrating investors who have been stopped out.

Professionals can see lists of stop loss orders waiting to be executed and can sell enough shares to trigger stops on as much as they want to buy at those lower prices. Wall Street traders "pick off" shares from novice investors with this tactic all the time.

Flash crashes can also affect a huge number of stocks and trigger automated stops in bunches. Prices can rebound in minutes, leaving you sold out of the market. Automated stops, like many things, are a two-edged sword with good aspects and bad aspects. How to use them is different for each investor.

Since I watch the market every day anyway, I avoid automated stops and instead use manual stop loss alerts to tell me to closely watch one of my stocks, and then execute my sells manually if warranted. If you can't or don't want to watch your stocks closely, go ahead and use automatic stops at your brokerage firm. The use of stops is so important that it outweighs the few disadvantages that I have mentioned.

Whenever you buy an investment, look at it and decide what would make you think it is no longer working and set a stop loss price based upon that evaluation.

CHAPTER 18 - THE BEST INVESTMENT VEHICLES

"Robo-advisers have not yet experienced a good down market in which to gauge their effectiveness. Until then, I equate automated advice services to rolling the dice. How lucky do you feel?"

Will Hepburn

If you were thinking I was going to tell you to buy the next Amazon, Google or Apple stock early in its rising trend, I am sorry to disappoint. In this chapter, I want to discuss different investment vehicles, or different ways to invest.

There are only two basic kinds of investments, debt - something that you are owed, and equity - something that you own. On paper, debt has lower risk because if a company goes under, the holders of its various forms of debt such as bonds, debentures, notes, etc., will get paid off before stockholders see a penny.

Stocks may seem like the most popular investment, but there is far more trading in the bond market than in stocks. And more yet in the currency markets. Dailyfx.com reports the volume of currencies traded on the Forex market, a decentralized global market where all the world's currencies trade. Forex is estimated to trade $4 trillion a day. This is more than five times larger than the global bond markets, which trade around $700 billion per day on average, and dwarfs the dollar volume of all the world's stock markets, which have a combined average only about $84 billion per day.

Since most of us leave currency and bond trading to the many banks, hedge funds, and institutional investors that account for most of the trading volume in those two markets, my comments here will focus primarily on stocks and other investments favored by retail investors such as yourself.

MUTUAL FUNDS

Mutual funds for several generations have been the favorite investment vehicle for the average investor. As the term *fund* suggests, these are pools of investor money where your investment is mingled with that of all other investors, unlike segregated investment accounts which have your name on each underlying investment. The pool is managed by a professional or team of professionals to achieve the goals stated in the fund's prospectus, freeing you to work, travel, spend time with your kids or whatever you might wish to do more than managing your investments.

You get instant diversification by investing in mutual funds because the pool of investments you buy into includes many stocks, bonds or whichever security the fund is focusing on.

Mutual funds are convenient in that they keep count in fractional shares, so you can add or withdraw any dollar amount of money at any time. This allows you to choose to reinvest dividends in additional fund shares, something you can't do with many other forms of investment. It also creates the ability for you to closely control your cash flow by asking that a certain dollar amount be sent to you each month. You get the check you expect, and the fund company's computers take care of selling just the right number of fractional shares to generate your distribution.

Drawbacks to owning mutual funds include:

End of day pricing. If you buy a fund during the day, you won't know exactly what you paid for it until the end of the day. The fund company has to add the value of all of its underlying investments and divide by the number of shares the fund has outstanding to get a net asset value per share, and the fund companies only do this once a day after the markets close. Generally, it will be several hours after trading stops when fund prices are posted.

Limited diversification. Although you will own a piece of many different investments through a mutual fund, most funds focus on a single asset class or market sector. You are responsible for ensuring that you have diversification across asset classes or look for a fund that uses multiple asset classes. These are called "go anywhere" funds. I like these because they free the fund manager to really manage your money. Most managers are very limited in their investment options by their prospectus. A go anywhere fund removes some of the manager's handcuffs.

You are also responsible for that final level of diversification, using different strategies. If you want out of the financial markets, say, during a bear market, or if you want to move to an investment with a different focus or style, you have to sell shares in the fund and move your assets elsewhere or instruct your financial adviser to do so. The fund typically won't do so without your directive.

Cost: Newer types of investments, specifically Exchange Traded Funds may have lower annual fees than traditional mutual funds.

Many mutual fund companies offer funds of funds. These are funds that invest in other investment funds. Investors inherently gain diversification by investing in multiple managers, strategies, or asset classes. You often see this tactic used by fund companies in target-date funds. In my opinion, funds of funds add needless layers of expense since there will be two fund management fees instead of one. You do get better diversification, though.

EXCHANGE TRADED FUNDS

Exchange Traded Funds, commonly called ETFs, trade like stocks, with continuous pricing throughout the day, but are similar to a mutual fund in that you buy into a pool of investments. ETFs do not have the same level of management as traditional mutual funds because they are required to follow a formula by which investments are selected and they can't stray from that formula. An index ETF will strive to stay in sync with a stock index such as the S&P 500, or one comprised just of energy stocks, emerging market stocks, etc. An entire industry has sprung up to develop arcane indexes for groups of investments to satisfy the requirements of esoteric ETFs.

Newer ETFs have begun utilizing formulas that follow market dynamics such as earnings or book values, so portfolios can be considered to have an active component even though they are driven by a formula.

ETFs have lower costs than traditional mutual funds and have moment-to-moment pricing throughout the day, but are a little less convenient. You cannot buy fractional shares of ETFs, so controlling the cash flow from ETFs does not work too well.

There is also a bid/ask spread on ETF pricing, similar to other types of stocks. You buy at the ask - the higher of the two prices - and sell at the bid or lower price. Making this small amount on each trade is how middlemen, called market makers, are encouraged to buy and sell shares and create or redeem shares to stabilize the market. Your shares have to increase in value by the amount of the spread before you can start to make a profit.

Most of the time, the spread is small, but occasionally it can widen. Wide spreads can occur on foreign stock ETFs bought in the U.S., because a market maker must issue you shares at the time of purchase but won't be able to offset his risk until the foreign markets open sometime later. If prices change on those foreign markets before they open, the ETF issuer can lose money, so this risk premium is added to the spread on the related ETF.

INDEX FUNDS

Index funds can be traditional mutual funds or ETFs and are designed to closely follow an index. They tend to become more popular the longer markets rise, as the memory of index losses during bear markets fade.

Some would say that it is hard to beat an index. In rising markets, it is hard but not impossible. There are two reasons for this. One is that indexes are managed to a certain extent. Companies within the indexes that fall on hard times are routinely replaced with newer, more growth-oriented companies.

The second reason is that a significant goal of proactive managers is not just to hit the lights out performance wise, but to reduce the risk of being invested. Every time a proactive manager makes a move to reduce risk and the market ignores that risk and charges ahead, the manager loses some performance relative to the index. A proactive manager's return lags a bit. This is the price of risk management. When a bear market does occur, however, proactive managers will often shine compared to index funds.

You pay for homeowner's insurance every year, but just because you don't have a fire doesn't mean you should cancel the insurance. Proactive management can be looked at like insurance on your portfolio. With it, you can have a degree of confidence that you won't ride a market all the way down, like the 56% loss some index fund investors took in 2007-09.

ROBO ADVISERS

Automated advice platforms are a new phenomenon, sometimes called robo-advice for your investments. These are programmed algorithms that automatically make changes in your accounts when required, freeing you from having to worry about management decisions, and also freeing you from dealing with those pesky brokers. Robo-advisers typically have very low fees since there is just a computer to pay for.

The allure of low fees and automatic decision making is compelling to many investors. I mean, who doesn't like softer, easier, and cheaper? These new investment vehicles have not yet been through a bear market, however. From what I know about them, they may not fare well during a sharp decline because they are largely programmed similarly, allocating portfolios according to Modern Portfolio Theory, and rebalancing the portfolios at certain times.

My concern about robos is that they are programmed to make investment decisions based on historic returns, expected correlations between investment classes, and a belief that all investors are average, which you know you are not. Robos can have little or no ability to adjust to events that have never happened before. How can you program something that has never happened into a computer?

Nassim Nicholas Taleb wrote a book called The Black Swan, with the premise that if you had never seen a black swan, because they live only in Australia, you could not know they exist. Therefore, you could not plan for it, because you can't even imagine there being one. His book is about unforeseen market events and was extremely timely - published in 2007 just a few months before the wheels started coming off the financial markets due to the collapse of the real estate and mortgage markets.

There is no human intervention in a robo-adviser to say "Whoa! This is different." I fear that the next black swan will be hard on the robo-advice industry.

Wall Street traders know how to use data that allows them to "pick off" novice investors by seeing orders waiting in the execution queues at the stock exchanges and taking advantage of the trades, and by extension, the investors in those trades. It is not much of a leap to imagine them deciphering robo-advice and front-running expected trades, making robos and their clients the rubes during market turbulence.

Early in my career, I learned that most investment defaults were in new enterprises that had not yet established themselves and survived a full market cycle.

As of this writing, robo-advisers are experiencing their first market correction. *InvestmentNews* reported on February 5, 2018 that the websites of two of the country's biggest robo-advisers, Wealthfront and Betterment, crashed as the S&P 500 Index sank 4.1%. If robos crash during such an ordinary market correction and have not yet experienced a real bear market in which to gauge their effectiveness, I equate automated advice services to rolling the dice. How lucky do you feel?

ANNUITIES

Annuities are the insurance industry's way of competing with bank CDs, mutual funds, etc., and can make investing very easy. They are often bought out of fear of losing money. Having an insurance company take that risk for you can be a nice comfort blanket. But there is a price. Usually that price is very high, so I am not a fan of annuities except for one use. Generating retirement income for investors without access to traditional retirement plans is an appropriate use for an annuity. However, to hold one as a long-term savings vehicle creates a tax bomb because at death, all the earnings will be taxed at the worst possible rate, as ordinary income, creating tax problems for your heirs.

The type of annuity sold at the free lunch seminars and in newspaper ads are almost always fixed, index-based annuities, meaning they will pay you a fixed return plus a portion of what a stock index produces. My experience is that it is hard to make more than a small fraction of what the stock markets produce when it all averages out. The insurance company keeps the rest. And the fees are horrendous, occasionally often high enough to drive you into negative returns despite the annuities being sold to prevent just that. Long lock-up periods enforced with exit fees are a reflection of the size of the commissions and fees you are paying.

If you look closely and can understand the details of an index annuity, you are pretty sharp. Many financial advisers can't even explain them properly, and if they are that complex there can be a lot of unknowns in them. Warren Buffett won't buy anything he can't understand, and my advice is neither should you.

REAL ESTATE INVESTMENT TRUSTS

Real Estate Investment Trusts, commonly called REITs, are just stocks that get a special tax treatment to make them work better for real-estate-oriented investors.

Some REITS are traded on the stock exchanges like regular stocks and usually pay a high dividend. The thing to watch out for is the proliferation of non-traded REITs sold by brokers, financial planners, and advisers. These have all the benefits of an exchange-traded REIT with one big drawback. They can't be sold. Since one thing we can count on when investing is change, either in the financial markets or in your personal life, the likelihood of you wanting to get out of a non-traded REIT is pretty good. However, the chances of you being able to sell are pretty poor. Non-traded REIT sponsors that make buy-back offers frequently can't make good on them, stranding their investors in frustrating, unproductive, or declining investments with no options.

There are many good ways to invest, and what might be good for one person might not feel so good to you. To say which vehicle is best depends very much on who you are speaking with.

Much of my work consists of making sure that my clients can be comfortable while their money is at work. There is only one thing that money is good for and that is not having to worry about money. There is simply no amount of money that is worth worrying about, so if you find yourself worrying about your investments, I would suggest that you find an investment adviser who can help you.

CHAPTER 19 - THOUGHTS WHEN SELECTING AN INVESTMENT ADVISER

"Investing is a life-long journey, choose your traveling companions carefully."

Will Hepburn

If you are like many readers of investment books, you probably have some aspect of either your investments or your investment advice that you are not entirely comfortable with and are looking to change. If that statement describes you, I would encourage you to not procrastinate but to take action.

Procrastination can be an expensive, sometimes even deadly malady. Consider the man who keeps putting off a trip to see his doctor about that strange pain he has had on and off for months. He always seems too busy, doesn't want to be seen as vulnerable, or is too frugal to pay for the visit, so it keeps getting put off, until it is too late, and the doctors tell him there is nothing they can do at this late stage.

Procrastination can ruin lives, but financial procrastination can devastate financial security and families, too.

A friend told me about a client that came to him in 2000 to do a comprehensive financial plan prior to a planned retirement. The client's main asset was $5,000,000 of Nortel stock. Nortel was the old Canadian Bell company. The tech boom was in full swing at the time, so the client was feeling pretty good financially. Due to scheduling conflicts the several meetings needed to create the financial plan were going to span a number of months, and the planner told the client he knew that part of his advice was going to be to liquidate the majority of the Nortel stock to diversify his investments and that the client should do so immediately due to the high-risk nature of his holding.

The client put off acting on the planner's advice and within a few weeks his $126 per share Nortel stock had lost 20% of its value, was on its way to a price of $6 within a few months, and ultimately went to zero in bankruptcy. Needless to say, that particular financial plan never did get done. Procrastination ruined not only this man's retirement but destroyed the financial security his family was depending on.

So, if something is bothering you about your finances, don't put off finding a solution any further. You must take action or nothing will change, and eventually the market may turn on you, too.

DO YOU NEED HELP?

If you are comfortable doing your own investment research and making your own investment decisions, and can sleep well while doing so, then you really don't need to pay for outside help with your investments. You can save money combining Internet research with discount brokers and calling fund companies on their 800 numbers to buy investments.

However, if you do need help with research or knowing what or when to buy or sell, or just aren't comfortable managing your money without some assistance, then you need to be ready to pay for that help. Working with a financial adviser can be a smart idea, and high net worth individuals are more likely to use advisers because the cost of making a mistake can be so high.

FIDUCIARY VERSUS NON-FIDUCIARY ADVISERS

Advisers come in two flavors, either fiduciary or non-fiduciary. The difference is something that you should understand because of the conflicts that can be caused by using the wrong type of adviser. Fiduciaries are required to act in your best interest and put your interests above their own. Non-fiduciaries are not held to this standard and can act in their own self-interest.

Commissioned brokers/planners/financial advisers are individuals licensed by FINRA, the Financial Industry Regulatory Authority, as Registered Representatives of an investment firm. All will be happy to help you because the more business they do the more money they make. They are compensated for their services by a commission, or a percentage of the investment's price. Once you have purchased your new investment, however, the adviser's incentive is not to keep advising you on it, but to find the next investor from whom he can earn a commission, so this type of compensation has a high conflict of interest.

I've heard brokers spin the disclosure of a commission by saying *"The company pays me, not you."* However, your money is the only money in play. Where do you think the company gets the money to write your adviser a paycheck? From you, because you are the only one with any money involved!

Rarely have I seen a commissioned adviser who is a true money manager. Almost all are salespeople of mutual funds, annuities or sometimes stocks but few are investment analysts or portfolio managers.

Their conflicts of interest will be disclosed in the fine print of the engagement agreement and may have wording similar to *"Our interests may not be the same as yours . . . we are paid by you, and sometimes by firms that compensate us based upon what you buy . . . our profits and our salespersons' compensation may vary by product and over time."* Wording of this type is a red flag about potential conflicts. Heed it if you want unbiased advice.

Complicating matters are the proliferation of accounts where for a flat annual fee you can have the services of the adviser. It doesn't feel like a commission because it is spread over many years, but the adviser is paid a percentage of your fee, or in other words, a commission. And the adviser's strongest motivation is to prospect for more clients rather than watch your money.

A Registered Representative of a brokerage firm represents the firm, not you and can be identified by the FINRA acronym in their disclosures. An adviser who can offer annuities is appointed as an agent of the company, not you. Ask about all the licenses your adviser has. These insights provide one more hint as to where allegiances may lie.

All of this is not to say that commissioned advisers cannot be fine people or deliver good advice, they can and often do. However, there are many conflicts along the way, and human nature being what it is, you need to understand the potential for problems before they crop up and before you invest your money.

Simply put, a fiduciary owes their allegiance to the person who pays them. If your adviser can be paid by someone other than you, their allegiance is to that person, not you. Fiduciaries are paid by you and only by you, and as a result owe their loyalty to you, not to a mutual fund company or a brokerage firm. As Bob Woodward said during the Watergate investigations, *"Follow the money."*

Registered Investment Adviser firms cannot accept commissions and are fiduciaries to their clients. Unfortunately, in the investment business hiding or disguising fees has become an art form, but a fiduciary will disclose all fees you will pay to them. I have seen clients blanch upon seeing the many fees in the investment world. There may be custodial fees for printing statements and providing online access, sending checks or a dozen other functions. If these fees are not itemized and disclosed, you are still paying them but with hidden fees.

If you want a fiduciary helping you with your investments and want to avoid all the conflicts that commissioned investing can bring, look for a Registered Investment Advisory firm to help you. Fee disclosure may be a little uncomfortable, but it is in your best interest.

QUESTIONS TO QUALIFY A PROSPECTIVE ADVISER

In the classes I teach, I often ask the students, *"Who wants an honest adviser?"* and every hand will go up. But how can you know? A simple way is to tell the prospective adviser that you are thinking of buying an annuity with your IRA money. The toe-stubber here is that your IRA is already tax sheltered. You don't need to pay an annuity company to provide a second layer of tax shelter because it does you no good, and an adviser will know this. However, annuities pay the highest commissions around. If the adviser goes along with your suggestion it is probably because they want to earn a fat commission regardless of whether the investment is really right for you. If this happens, you might want to find another adviser.

Another good question to ask when shopping for advisers is *"What is their plan for dealing with a bear market or a recession?"* The harsh light of this question can tell you if you have an adviser who is just a salesperson or one who can really add value in tough times. Sadly, many advisers are great talkers, but are clueless about protecting money in tough times.

Successful investing is not a one-decision process, it never has been. Sitting back and doing nothing while markets change is not a plan - it is the lack of a plan no matter what it is called! If your adviser will not be doing much to earn his/her fee or commissions, it might be time for you to look elsewhere. If you have taken losses or underperformed the markets, you can't undo the past, but you can certainly do something about your future. Investing is a life-long journey, choose your traveling companions carefully.

CHAPTER 20 - SCAMS AND OTHER PITFALLS

" . . . while professional designations often imply a degree of special training or experience of some extent, they can also be used as a marketing or self-promotional hook. Be wary of financial professionals who make too much of their designation or try to tout their designation as the reason you should hire them. A professional designation should never be the sole reason you select an investment professional."

FINRA, The Financial Industry Regulatory Authority

Although the premise of this book is that almost all investments begin their life being good investments that are set adrift among the changing currents of the investment markets and end up mashed up on the rocks of a declining market, there are a few investments that never get that far down the road to being decent investments. These are the scams and pitfalls of investing. Before we end our conversation, I want to touch on them here.

In speaking engagements around the country, one of my two favorite presentations is called the **Top Ten Investment Scams and How to Avoid Them.** (The other favorite is Investing in Future Technologies). The Top 10 Scams talks are modeled from an annual report published by the National Association of State Securities Administrators on the topic.

DON'T TRUST, VERIFY

There is a website run by FINRA, the Financial Industry Regulatory Authority, Inc., that every investor should use to check out their financial adviser, called **BrokerCheck**. You can enter the name of the firm or your adviser and in seconds see their regulatory history. If your prospective adviser has had a string of complaints, lawsuits or settlements of claims, perhaps you would be wise to keep looking before you become a statistic. You can try it out yourself at www.Brokercheck.com.

A somewhat similar site is available for registered investment advisers under the auspices of the Securities and Exchange Commission - the **Investment Adviser Public Disclosure** website at www.adviserinfo.sec.gov/. This website will also search FINRA's BrokerCheck system and indicate whether an entity is a Brokerage firm.

Don't be afraid to ask the adviser about who makes the investment decisions. Is it the adviser you know or some faceless person back in New York? And ask to see their past recommendations. Most salespeople will tell you what you should buy now, usually based upon what has been working well recently. But what you really want to know is what he sold his clients just before a big decline in the markets, such as 2008, and how those investments did during the market decline or how he managed the movement of investment money out of harm's way. Few salespeople will have that data available. Money managers keep records of every trade they have made and will be able to show you recommendations made in various periods.

PENNY STOCKS

Everyone likes a bargain, ensuring that penny stocks always make my list of Top 10 scams. After all, how much can someone lose if they only invest 50 cents a share. The fallacy here is that one should not count investment returns in dollars (or cents), but in percentages. That way you can compare a $1 investment to a $100,000 investment using the same yardstick.

Obviously, one problem making it so difficult for penny stock investors to make profits is that many tiny companies whose stock is valued at only a buck or two, or less, will go out of business. Common wisdom is that only one out of five new businesses survive and remain in business for five years. So, buying penny stocks is a little like rolling the dice.

However, the more constant drag on penny stock profits is the spread between the bid and ask prices. When you look at *The Wall Street Journal* or the Internet for a stock price there are two prices presented, one at which you sell, called the bid price, and one at which you buy, called the ask price. The spread between those two prices is what middle men, called market makers, earn for standing ready with an inventory of shares to sell to you at the ask price, and stand ready with a basket of cash to buy shares from you at the bid price. It works like a wholesale/retail markup at the grocery store. When Safeway buys a case of Wheaties, they markup their cost to "the ask" price before putting boxes on the shelf to sell to you. Stocks work the same way.

If you see the penny stock of XYZ company with a bid-ask spread of $0.10 to $0.25, that is only 15 cents per share, which may seem cheap. In comparison, Domino's Pizza shares at this writing are sporting an 18 cent spread. So, what's the problem?

If you buy XYZ, you will need to wait until the bid price, currently 10 cents, has risen above the ask price that you paid, 25 cents, before you get to put any profit in your pocket. Remembering the math of gains and losses, we can see that to earn 15 cents on a 10 cent base requires a 150% profit. How easy is it to earn 150% on an investment? Not easy.

In contrast, Domino's Pizza had a bid-ask spread of $187.26 to $187.44, an 18 cent spread. However, to earn 18 cents on a $187 base amount is only a 1/10%, which is a lot easier to earn back. On which stock are you more likely to turn a profit? The one needing only a 1/10% gain or a huge 150% gain?

Spreads are a measure of liquidity. The narrower the spread, percentage-wise, the more buyers are willing to put money into Wall Street's cash register, so you can take it out on a sale. Big spreads are required to attract money to illiquid investments. Other illiquid investments such as gold or silver coins face this same bid/ask spread problem. Big spreads are a constant headwind for illiquid investments, so don't overlook spreads.

PUMP AND DUMP SCHEMES

Several years ago, I was leaving a hotel and saw an investment seminar beginning. Always looking for new ways to present old ideas, I thought I would sit in on this one to see what I could learn. It turned out to be a teaser meeting to get investors to sign up for a three-day class on trading techniques. The promoters promised to bring in past seminar graduates who had become millionaires with this company's strategy. The cost was only $3,900 for the three-day class, and you were guaranteed to make more than the tuition or your money cheerfully refunded.

My BS meter was racing off the charts with this presentation for several reasons. First, in the investment business when everyone starts to do the same thing the balance between buyers and sellers - that is what a market is all about - will shift and what they are all doing will stop making money. For this reason, really successful investors guard their secrets and rarely let anyone see into their black box of decision making. Why would millionaire investors offer to train a bunch of rookies, I wondered?

The promoters offered to show how stocks were chosen for consideration with live internet pricing projected for the class, complete with charts showing investments hitting buy point triggers at which time the presenter would execute a purchase of shares in his own account right there in front of the class. The promoters were so gracious that they would even provide a bank of computers in the back of the classroom so students could piggyback on the presenter's expertise and do their own trades if they wanted.

That is when my alarm bells really went off. This was a really slick *pump and dump* scheme.

Pump and dumps are ways unscrupulous promoters generate interest in stocks they own and then sell their shares into the rising wave of interest at higher and higher prices. Generally, the focus is on small illiquid companies, often penny stocks, whose prices can be moved upward with a small amount of investment. It is not uncommon for prices to be driven up 1000% during these feeding frenzies by greedy, naive investors. As the promotion ends, buying interest slowly dries up and the price drifts back down to its earlier level after the promoter moves on to a new town, a new stock, and a new bunch of suckers.

In this case, I was sure the promoter's associates, friends and relatives all knew what stock would be purchased that day and had loaded up on it before the transaction was done on stage. As students ran to computers in the back to enter their buys, the class could see with their own eyes the price rising. Calls would be made to friends and families of students to buy, buy! Of course, more buys would happen and the price would rise for a few days as word got around confirming the presenters' skills. Then the class would be over, and the inevitable deflation of expectations and bank accounts would begin.

WORTHLESS NEWSLETTERS

Another investment pitfall is the investment newsletter writers who often mimic the style of the *National Enquirer* generating a lot of fuss over nothing. Mundane topics such as dividend reinvestment can be presented as the latest, greatest discovery since the Internet. Only after paying a subscription fee do you get the dramatically presented strategy guidelines, then realize it is really pretty ho-hum stuff. If you really want more sexy, sure fire ways to strike it rich, they often have another newsletter to sell you and another, and another. Some outfits have a dozen newsletters to offer, each more inflammatory or specialized than the previous one. And total costs can easily run into the thousands of dollars. It is really a sales scam.

Often the topics newsletters tout are story stocks that make companies or industries sound oh-so good, with oh-so much potential that little details like lack of earnings and sales are glossed over. The tech bubble of the late 1990s was known for stocks that had no earnings or sales being driven to absurd levels by waves of publicity. As the tech-laden Nasdaq index dropped 78% of its value after March 2000 and took 16.5 years to overcome those losses, the lesson of not chasing story stocks sunk in. Tesla may be the next stock market darling to be exposed as merely a story stock. Stay tuned for that one.

These stories can be so compelling that even conservative, octogenarians can get sucked in. In early 2008, I lost a big client who was an elderly lady in an assisted living facility who kept bringing me cockamamie ideas from newsletters like this. After I shot down the ideas enough times, she fired me, and I assume followed the newsletter recommendations instead. I fear that her net worth took a big hit as the financial crisis unfolded.

Someone once likened these tabloid style newsletters to pornography. They leave you excited and confused.

WORTHLESS DESIGNATIONS

One of the dirty little secrets of the investment profession is that it takes no particular education or credentials to be registered or licensed as a financial adviser. Just pay $155 and get a 72% score or better on the 130-question test and you can say you are a financial adviser.

The value in having an adviser is not just having one, but the knowledge and experience that person brings to the table.

You will find many advisers with a string of letters after their name. Chances are that alphabet soup refers to one or more professional designations showing various levels of experience and education. It would be good for you to know that there is a big difference in simply being registered and having professional designations.

In general, professional designations are a good thing, a way to let investors know which professionals have certain skill levels. Continuing education requirements may ensure that they stay educated and have made the commitment to learning. This is all well and good and benefits you.

However, while designations imply special training or experience of some extent, they can also be used as a marketing or self-promotional hook. In fact, an industry has sprung up to generate and sell designations, many of which are worthless but look good after someone's name. Some designations can get obtained with a few hours spent on the Internet and, of course, a fee paid to the sponsoring organization.

FINRA, the Financial Industry Regulatory Authority, now lists 178 different designations that they recognize, which is almost four times the number reported in 2005. You can access their Professional Designation Database at www.finra.org/investors/professional-designations to find out the requirements for a designation.

All financial designations are not created equal. Some involve fairly rigorous standards to earn and maintain the designation and allow investors to verify the status of anyone claiming to hold that designation. A few even have a formal disciplinary process. Others are relatively easy to earn and might be maintained by simply paying a yearly fee. Go to FINRA's Professional Designation Database to find out which designations have some validity.

Keep in mind that while professional designations often imply a degree of special training or experience of some extent, they can also be used as a way to hype the skills of the adviser. Be wary of financial professionals who make too much of their designations or try to tout their designations as the reason you should hire them. A professional designation should never be the sole reason you select an investment professional.

Designations can be faked. Sadly, like any credential, a financial designation can be used by fraudsters to build credibility and gain trust by claiming to be an expert or have a special designation—a tactic known as source credibility. But credibility can be faked.

Many organizations that issue financial designations provide the public with a database of those who hold an up-to-date designation (you can find web links to conduct such a search using the previously mentioned Professional Designations database). It's a good policy to ask anyone who claims to hold a designation when they earned it and whether it's still current—and then, if possible, verify with the issuing organization that this is truly the case.

FINRA suggests you always look at their BrokerCheck website at https://brokercheck.finra.org/ to **do research on your prospective adviser and see whether they are, in fact, registered, hold designations or have a history of complaints against them.**

According to the book Investing for Dummies, many credentials with the word "senior" or "retirement" in them are next to worthless.

Out of all the 178 designations recognized by FINRA, I consider perhaps five or six to be worthwhile. The designations that would be of interest to you as a retail investor and are most respected and recognized by the financial industry and the media include:

- Chartered Financial Analyst (CFA) certification
- Certified Public Accountant (CPA) certification
- Certified Financial Planner (CFP) designation
- Chartered Life Underwriter (CLU) and
- Chartered Financial Consultant (ChFC)
- Chartered Market Technician (CMT)

All others should be considered as bling for a business card because their courses of study are much less rigorous. I can testify to this because I was a financial adviser for many years. In 1994, I decided to get the Certified Financial Planner shingle because I figured I was already doing the work, so why not?

Was I ever surprised by how much I did not know when I took the six grad-school-level courses which were needed just to qualify to take the two-day CFP exam. I practiced as a Certified Financial Planner for many years, with 30 hours of continuing education required every two years, so I can attest to how much CFPs are required to know.

COMMON CHARACTERISTICS OF A SCAM

Scam artists prey on us continually, especially in bad times. The story and wrapper on the scams may change, but some things are usually present within fraudulent schemes and can alert you to a possible scam. They are:

- The offering of an unregistered security.

  All securities, including stocks, bonds, and notes, must be registered with the Securities and Exchange Commission (SEC) before they can be offered for sale to the public. Registered securities can be found in the SEC EDGAR database.

- No daily pricing available on Yahoo, *The Wall Street Journal* or other public venue.

No daily pricing typically means no liquidity or way to sell your investment.

♦ The absence of independent custodians to hold your money or securities.

NEVER (1) write a check, and/or (2) transfer your assets to your financial adviser directly. All checks and all assets should only be transferred to the client's own named and numbered account held at a financially secure, well-respected custodian that is independent of their individual financial adviser. Bernie Madoff was able to steal more than $18 billion in client assets because he owned the custodian which theoretically held those assets. The purpose of a custodial relationship is to separate the "holding and safeguarding" of an investor's assets from the financial adviser so that nobody can get access to the investor's assets without their consent. Your adviser may direct trades in your account, but cannot access the funds.

♦ No SIPC/FDIC insurance. SIPC/FDIC insurance is something to insist upon for your investments. The insurance does not protect you from market losses but does protect you from the financial failure of the custodian, bank or brokerage firm.

SIPC (Securities Investor Protection Corporation) protects assets in brokerage accounts of SIPC-member broker-dealers if the firm fails financially. Coverage is up to $500,000 per customer for all accounts at the same institution, including a maximum of $250,000 for cash. FDIC (Federal Deposit Insurance Corporation) insurance protects your assets in a bank account - checking or savings - up to a maximum of $250,000 per owner. Member firms pay premiums for the insurance coverage.

CHAPTER 21 - IN CLOSING

"Proactive investing is an all-weather form of investing. But you need to be the one to decide when it is time to come in out of the rain."

Will Hepburn

If after reading this book you have decided that you want the benefits that proactive investing can provide for your financial future, your next decision is whether to do the investment management yourself or hire a professional money manager to help you.

Naturally, you can save money by doing the decision making yourself. After all, professionals all charge a fee, with the majority charging a flat annual rate that varies with the amount you have invested. Proactive investing may not be the least expensive way to go because the fees of proactive managers reflect the relatively intense oversight given to your money compared to ordinary financial advisers. Think of a proactive manager's fee like you think of collision insurance on your car, you hope you never really need it, and you continue to pay it just in case. At those few times it is really needed, you are sooo grateful that you have it.

If you think you would prefer a performance-based fee, such as a fee based upon a portion of profits made in your account, thinking this will even better align your interests with those of the money manager, that decision is not as simple as you might think. If a manager is close to the point where he will make a fee or not, his incentive changes from achieving your objective, limited by how much risk you were willing to take, to achieving his objective, which is getting paid and saving his job. This conflict of interest may encourage the manager to take added risks to clear the hurdle between him and his fee, risks beyond what you agreed to at the outset of your relationship. He might be tempted to roll the dice for you, and at that point, your interests may no longer be aligned as well as you thought when you asked for a performance-based fee.

PROACTIVELY MANAGING YOUR OWN PORTFOLIO

If you want to save investment management fees by calling the shots yourself that is understandable and doable by many investors. You will still need a brokerage firm to hold your portfolio while it is invested. I would suggest that you look for a discount brokerage that is paid for executing trades quickly and inexpensively without providing investment advice.

The online brokerage community has grown tremendously in the last few years, which is great for investors who want to easily and cost effectively participate in online trading of stocks, ETFs and mutual funds. The competition has forced innovation, cheap online stock trades, and additional features such as education and training centers, charting software, videos, free webinars, chat rooms and forums, social networking, free tax software to track gains and losses, and more. So, plenty of resources are there for you.

A quick Internet search will bring up a list of potential discount brokers who can handle your accounts. To determine which one is right for you, I suggest evaluating your trading habits and needs, and comparing various features available at these firms such as:

- ◆ Available investments
- ◆ Account types (IRA, taxable accounts, 529 plans, trusts, banking services, and more)
- ◆ Commissions (cost per trade)
- ◆ Options trading (availability, and cost per option)
- ◆ Online only vs. brick and mortar offices where you can get face to face with an adviser
- ◆ Availability of broker-assisted trades
- ◆ Fees for account maintenance, IRA custody, issuing checks or bank transfers, etc.
- ◆ Education and investment training
- ◆ Charting software
- ◆ Tax software for tracking investments, capital gains and tax-loss harvesting

♦   Customer service

One piece of advice I will give you is to start small. If your accounts have been in passively held investments, don't transfer 100% to a proactive account, start with a small part of your savings to be sure you want to and have the temperament and skills to proactively invest yourself. As you get more comfortable with handling your own accounts add to the proactive side of your portfolio. Remember, buy and hold has its place in a diversified portfolio but should not be 100% of anyone's portfolio, in my opinion.

And, if you find yourself getting nervous as the markets start to change and signs of a market reversal begin to mount, don't be afraid to turn the management of your accounts over to a seasoned professional. There is no amount of money worth worrying about, and in a bear market a professional proactive money manager is just about the best security blanket there is. Know that it is OK to change your mind about handling your money yourself. Proactive investing is an all-weather form of investing, but you need to be the one to decide when it is time to come in out of the rain.

FINDING A PROACTIVE MONEY MANAGER

One place to start looking for a proactive money manager should you decide you want one is the National Association of Active Investment Managers (NAAIM). NAAIM is not large, but it is an elite group of active managers who regularly meet for training and education in proactive management. The association has a Find An Adviser resource on its website that will let you look for proactive managers by state or firm name - www.naaim.org/resources/find-an-advisor/

If you need one more resource, I would welcome your questions at Invest@HepburnCapital.com

May the majority of your trades be winners
(don't expect to get them all right).

May the majority of your losses be small
(know when to cut your losses and live to invest another day).

May all your diversification be effective.

And, may you live without economic insecurity because you know
***Why Bad Things Happen to Good Investments**.*

Good investing to you!

Will Hepburn

APPENDIX - INVESTOR RESOURCES

RESOURCES LIST

- **Brokercheck.com**. This site can tell you instantly whether a person or firm is registered, as required by law, to sell securities (stocks, bonds, mutual funds and more), offer investment advice or both. BrokerCheck gives you a snapshot of a broker's employment history, licensing information and regulatory actions, arbitrations, and complaints.
- **IAPD - Investment Adviser Public Disclosure** website. www.adviserinfo.sec.gov. You can search for a Registered Investment Adviser firm on this website and view the registration or reporting form (Form ADV) that the adviser filed to register with the SEC and/or the states. Form ADV contains information about an investment adviser and its business operations. Additionally, it contains disclosure about certain disciplinary events involving the adviser and its key personnel.
- **Investopedia.** A wide range of Investment topics and news. If you are brand new to investing, start with their Investing 101 Tutorial
- ***Investor's Business Daily.*** Online or as a print newspaper. Educational and provides great tools for stock selection plus reports on pre-screened stocks
- **Finance.Yahoo.com.** Input your investments into a custom portfolio to follow them during the day.
- **StockCharts.com**, **BigCharts.com**, and **FreeStockCharts.com**. All offer many free charting tools and tutorials.
- **FinViz.com**. An excellent and comprehensive stock screening tool.

- **AAII**. Resources to help start a local investment club.
- **NAAIM.** The National Association of Active Investment Managers. NAAIM.org. See their stock market Exposure Index at https://www.naaim.org/programs/naaim-exposure-index/ Contact NAAIM.org to find an active investment manager in your area. http://www.naaim.org/resources/find-an-advisor/

BOOKS ON INVESTING

- Rich Dad, Poor Dad (2000), by Robert Kiyosaki. (*Disclosure, I provided some of the material used in this book and Robert lists me in the acknowledgements section.*)
- Beating the Street, (1994), by Peter Lynch, one of the most successful stock market investors and mutual fund managers of the 20th century.
- The Intelligent Investor (1949), by Benjamin Graham, the father of value investing and one of Warren Buffett's teachers.
- Think and Grow Rich (1937) by Napoleon Hill. A classic that has sold over 30 million copies, provides insights into the psychology of success and abundance.
- Intermarket Analysis, Profiting from Global Market Relationships (2011), by John Murphy. Defines reasons why equity, bond, currency, and commodity markets move in relation to one another.
- Technical Analysis of the Financial Markets (1999), by John Murphy.
- The Little Book of Stock Market Cycles (2012), by Jeffery Hirsch
- Stock Charts for Dummies (2018) by Greg Schnell and Lita Epstein

LIST OF TABLES

LIST OF FIGURES

INDEX

Made in USA - North Chelmsford, MA
1052303_9780692069035
03.04.2020 1558